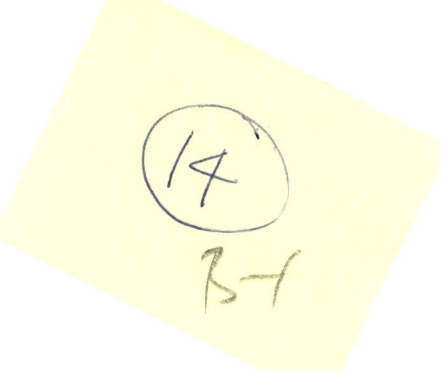

The Human Form Divine

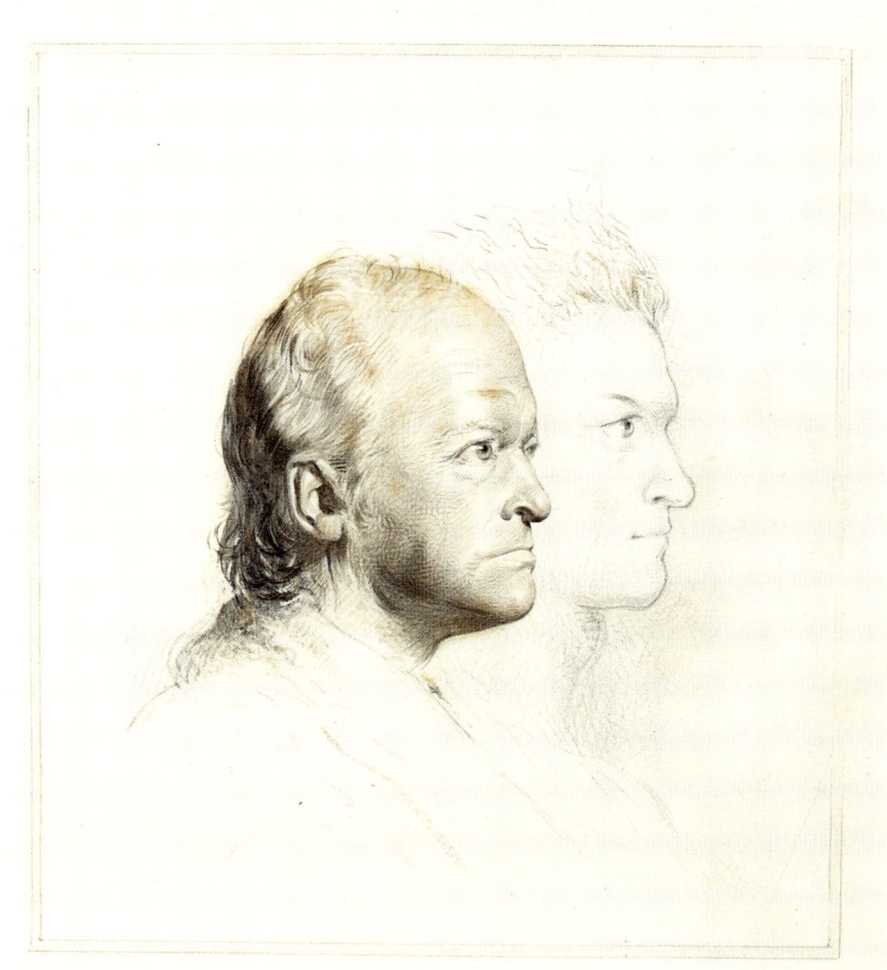

Portraits of
Willm Blake
at the ages of 28 & 69 years.

Born November 20th 1757.   Died August 12. 1827
Ætat: 69.

The Human Form Divine

William Blake from the Paul Mellon Collection

Patrick Noon

YALE CENTER FOR BRITISH ART
YALE UNIVERSITY PRESS
NEW HAVEN AND LONDON

Frontispiece: George Richmond, after Frederick Tatham,
William Blake in Youth and Old Age,
graphite with brush and brown ink, c. 1830.

Published on the occasion of an exhibition at the Yale Center for British Art,
New Haven, Connecticut, 2 April through 6 July 1997.

Copyright © 1997 by Yale University.
All rights reserved.
This book may not be reproduced, in whole or in part, including illustrations, in any form
(beyond that copying permitted by Sections 107 and 108 of the U.S. Copyright Law and except
by reviewers for the public press), without written permission from the publishers.

Designed by Lisa C. Tremaine
Set in Dante and Poetica by Yale University Printing and Graphic Services
Printed in the United States of America by Thames Printing

Library of Congress Cataloging-in-Publication Number 97-60263
ISBN 0-300-07174 (cloth: alk. paper)
ISBN 0-930606-81-7 (paper: alk. paper)

A catalogue record for this book is available from the British Library.

The paper in this book meets the guidelines for permanence and durability of the Committee
on Production Guidelines for Book Longevity of the Council on Library Resources.

10 9 8 7 6 5 4 3 2 1

CONTENTS

Preface   vii

Introduction   1

Chronology   13

Plates   17

Catalogue   75

    Illuminated Books   76

    Temperas   79

    Watercolors and Drawings   79

    Prints   82

    Illustrated Books with Engravings by or after Blake   84

    Related Material   85

References and Select Bibliography   87

PREFACE

William Blake is both central to and an eccentric part of the design of English art and literature. His very originality as an artist frequently makes him appear profoundly idiosyncratic, directed by his own visionary impulse. Yet we know from modern scholarship and criticism how deep are his debts to other artists and writers, from Michelangelo and Raphael to Shakespeare and contemporary eighteenth-century poets. The more closely we examine the context of late eighteenth- and early nineteenth-century British art, the more we find counterparts to his distinctive interests among such contemporaries as James Barry and John Hamilton Mortimer. Although public failure and obscurity dogged his days as an artist, he developed an intense and loyal group of followers that included Samuel Palmer and John Linnell. Yet he stands alone, distinct and hard to assimilate. "He was naked and saw man naked, and from the center of his own crystal," wrote T. S. Eliot in his sharp early characterization.

If Blake continues to attract the scholarship of art historians and to excite the interests of literary critics, he also continues to shape contemporary practice in both art and literature. Allen Ginsberg is but the most prominent of his recent followers. Perhaps what attracts an intense following of Blake beyond the academy is his reaction against an age of reason. He is seen as a pilgrim of the absolute, driven by a visionary passion both religious and sensual.

His own well-known reactions against reason, against the positivism of his age, are vividly articulated in the angry marginalia scribbled in his copy of Sir Joshua Reynolds' *Discourses*: "Artists who are above a plain Understanding are mock'd and Destroy'd by this President of Fools." And on the same page Blake declares, "What has reasoning to do with the Art of Painting?"

The paradoxes of William Blake cannot be easily dispelled, however, into rational versus irrational, reason versus intuition, the world of appearance versus a world of the visionary imagination. It is easy to imagine him a prophet of a new age, and we are wise to hearken to F. R. Leavis' stern warning: "The notion that by a devout study of Blake's symbolism a key can be found that will open to us a supreme esoteric wisdom is absurd; and to emphasize in that spirit the part played in his life's work by Swedenborg, Boehme, Paracelsus, Orphic tradition, Gnosticism and a 'perennial philosophy' is to deny what makes him important."

For Blake is the poet and painter deeply rooted in his place and in his time. The newly found America and the French Revolution form part of his radical view of the world. London is where his vision takes hold.

> *What are those golden builders doing? Where was the*
> *burying place*
> *Of soft Ethinthus? Near Tyburn's fatal Tree? Is that*

*Mild Zion's hill's most ancient promontory, near mournful
Ever weeping Paddington?*

The specificity of Blake, the succession of realized forms and images, lies at the center of his achievement as artist and poet. For Blake, particularity was both aesthetic and ethic. "Particular detail is the Foundation of the Sublime," he wrote. "He who would do good to another must do it in Minute Particulars."

Because so much of Blake's art lies in the illuminated books and in the watercolors, drawings, and prints, and cannot be permanently displayed for reasons of conservation, we are able to show the collection only in special exhibitions. The advantage is that Blake's images fall on us with the force of freshness. Their Minute Particulars strike with the vigor of their original conception and are not dulled by familiarity or repetition.

The collection of William Blake at the Yale Center for British Art, lovingly assembled over many years by Paul Mellon, is a hidden reservoir of form and feeling. Patrick Noon, curator of prints, drawings, and rare books, eloquently tells the story of the Blake collection in this catalogue. Mr. Mellon's delight in and understanding of the artist led to the formation of one of the most beautiful and intimate of all Blake collections. It points to one further paradox.

In 1936, Paul Mellon bought his first oil painting: presciently, it was George Stubbs's *Pumpkin and Stable Hand* (1774). In his own words he was "bowled over by the charming horse, the young boy in a cherry-colored jacket and the beautiful landscape background." William Blake was Mr. Mellon's second enthusiasm in British art. Although Stubbs was born thirty-three years before Blake, significant portions of their careers overlap. This fact is surprising, for they seem to stand at opposite poles of British art. Stubbs is the perfect eye, where pictorial truthfulness lies in fidelity to observation. Blake is the supreme poet and painter of the inner life. Yet we know that Blake saw a painting of a "Tyger" by Stubbs when he was a youth at Henry Pars's Drawing School. Both artists were to frame its fearful symmetry. Both knew that "the wrath of the lion is the wisdom of God." Where better to see and experience that profound affinity than in the Paul Mellon collection at the Yale Center for British Art?

Patrick McCaughey

INTRODUCTION

*Nations are Destroy'd, or Flourish, in proportion as Their Poetry
Painting and Music, are Destroy'd or Flourish!*
—WILLIAM BLAKE, *Jerusalem*

The graphic arts collections of the Yale Center for British Art constitute a repository of such richness and depth that their assemblage in just a few decades during the third quarter of this century is a feat which continues to astound visitors and specialists alike. Two names loom in the recounting of this story: Paul Mellon, whose benefactions in the arts have exceeded most norms of twentieth-century philanthropy, and William Blake, whose own world of archetypal giants partially inspired the program of acquisition that culminated in the founding of this unique cultural asset. The centrality of Blake to the Mellon collection, however, is rarely apparent. Only one of his paintings is on permanent view in the Center's galleries. The casual visitor to the museum is treated to the serenity of George Stubbs's sporting art, to a banquet of landscape painters of which Turner, Constable, and Bonington fix the parameters of romantic naturalism with authority and profusion, to an arresting and unexpected ensemble of Ben Nicholson's still-life constructions—all of which underscore the expansiveness of Paul Mellon's vision and the singularity of his accomplishment. But the stalwart and scholar alone tend to venture beyond the public spaces into the Study Room, where the whole of Blake's universe occupies a bank of oak cabinets awaiting a more intimate reading. The following remarks and catalogue mean to introduce to a larger audience the entirety of the Center's Blake collection, while briefly examining its principal pieces and formation and its relation to the other components of the Mellon donation.

When Paul Mellon and his curators began seriously to acquire British art in the 1960s, they had the good fortune and unusual acumen of plunging into an area of collecting that was much undervalued internationally and very much the private preserve of a handful of passionate but ageing British gentlemen. Possibly as many as one-third of the Center's fifty thousand watercolors, drawings, and prints and twenty thousand rare books originated in a discrete number of private collections, each representing the life's work of an individual connoisseur or bibliophile, each unique in its character and appeal. They represent an irreducible nucleus of quality around which the remainder of the collections have been assembled.

At the heart of the watercolor collection, for instance, are the several thousand sheets acquired from five distinguished amateurs. The earliest and largest group of drawings came between 1962 and 1973 from Leonard G. Duke, whose surviving manuscript ledger reveals a fascinating preoccupation with issues of authenticity and a voracious acquisitiveness of which bartering and bargain hunting were the lineaments. Next in numerical importance, but arguably the more aesthetically significant, is the collection in part assembled and in part inherited by Tom Girtin, the descendant and namesake of the great romantic watercolor painter Thomas Girtin (1775–1802). It was acquired in 1970 and was followed three years later by the collections of Martin Hardie and Iolo Williams, both of whom had published histories of British watercolor painting in the 1960s that remain fundamental texts within the ever more sophisticated literature on the subject. The final member of this core quintet is Thomas E. Lowinsky, whose collection, acquired in 1975, contained many fine specimens of figure drawing, including Blake's *Study for a Destroying Deity*.[1] Given the preference of all these collectors for the tranquil imagery of landscape watercolor painting, it should not surprise that the only other Blake drawings among their collective holdings were three small landscape sketches in the Duke collection executed during Blake's period at Felpham—that "sweet place for study," as he described William Hayley's (1745–1820) estate near Chichester—and Iolo Williams's iconic wash drawing *Moses Receiving the Law,* in which the influence of John Flaxman (1755–1826), Blake's "Sublime Archangel and Companion from Eternity," is less apparent than in most other related Old Testament illustrations that mark Blake's advent as an artist in about 1780.

An equally illustrious constellation of names defines the character of the print and book collections. In 1970, Mr. Mellon rescued from the oblivion of the Morgan Library's reserve storage a group of fifteen hundred mezzotint engravings. J. Pierpont Morgan and his legendary curator Belle da Costa Greene had scoured the international print trade for the better part of four decades at the beginning of this century in search of the most beautiful and rarest examples of this exquisite but fragile medium. The bounty of their efforts is indisputably the most important collection of mezzotints in North America. An important archive of Shakespeare iconography and of historical painting entered the collections in 1976 with the acquisition of nearly five hundred reproductive engravings that represented the teaching collection of Lincoln Kirstein's American Shakespeare Theater in Stratford, Connecticut. In the same year the limitless variety of J. M. W. Turner's genius was honored with the purchase of two encyclopedic collections of prints, by and after the artist, that had been assembled independently. The more definitive of the two is that of Sir Stephan Courtauld, who acquired his two thousand prints in 1919 from the great Turner historian W. G. Rawlinson. Line engravings and countless touched and annotated proofs constitute the bulk of the Courtauld horde.

The emphasis of the rare book collection is on illustrated books, and its foundation is the magnificent library of Major J. R. Abbey, whose two thousand volumes of "color-plate" books remain the standard bibliography on British scenery, travel, and customs between 1750 and 1850. The library of Rupert Gunnis, author of a *Dictionary of British Sculptors* (1951), admirably complements the Abbey holdings as it traces British genealogy, architecture, and local history over four centuries. A more curious trove are the twenty-four hundred leaves, assembled by Fred Werther of Baltimore, which attempt to chart the history of the arts of printing and illustration on the continent between 1450 and 1600. It represents the industry of three hundred European printers and the elite of Northern woodcut artists, from Albrecht Dürer to Hans Baldung Grien. In the grandness of its pretensions and the stamp of its contents, it is a collection that would have enchanted Blake.[2]

In his autobiography, Paul Mellon writes candidly of his acquisitive practices:

> *I have been a collector of collections when opportunity has arisen. This might seem a symptom of greed or at best an indiscriminate appropriation of widely different and incompatible congeries of books, pictures, sculptures, or other objects of art. To this charge I plead innocent, for in each purchase of a whole collection I have always had a probable or possible eventual repository in mind. Not only that, but in every case it has seemed an opportunity of a lifetime and almost a duty to prevent the dispersal of the collection in question. It bothered me to think of beautiful objects or literary treasures, which had always been kept together, being sold one by one, never to be reassembled.*[3]

This desire to preserve and juxtapose intact collections has always been a characteristic of Mr. Mellon's collecting designs. It informed his purchase in 1959 of the eight hundred surviving volumes of John Locke's library and its subsequent donation to the Bodleian Library at Oxford; his purchases for the British Art Center, well after it opened in 1977, of Stubbs's Comparative Anatomical drawings and Turner's breathtaking "Channel" sketchbook, both of which were destined by the art trade to be disbound and sold by the sheet; the acquisition of Blake's radiant watercolor illustrations of the poems of Thomas Gray (1716–1771), which were also saved from this desecration by a timely private treaty; and most obviously, his gathering together for the Study Room of the British Art Center the numerous separate collections previously described, which cohere into a curiously staccato yet compelling narrative of British invention in the graphic arts.

But the one group of works at Yale that uniquely joins the many strands of Paul Mellon's private interests and experiences—his passion for books and for British Art, which date from the 1930s; his formative years at Yale, when he was privileged to study with such legendary mentors as Chauncey Brewster Tinker, Fred Pottle, and Clyde de Vane; and his admiration for esoteric traditions in western intellectual thought—is not the legacy of some other admired collector, plucked from the market during the heady years of buying immediately leading up to the opening of the British Art Center. Rather, it is the rich collection of William Blake's Illuminated Books, paintings, and engravings, which Mr. Mellon assembled piecemeal and entirely according to his own tastes over a lifetime of appreciative involvement with Blake's poetry and art. In those terms, it might be viewed as *the* core collection, and its history is not lacking scholarly and anecdotal interest.

Paul Mellon began to build his private library while studying at Cambridge in the 1930s. His initial purchases were "color-plate" and sporting books. Of Blake he has recalled that "his haunting poetry with its arcane mythology and his beautiful illuminated books have always held a special appeal to me,"[4] so it was perhaps inevitable that he would venture into Blake collecting at the comparatively early date of 1941. The largest exhibition of Blake's work ever organized in North America had also just closed at the Philadelphia Museum of Art and had done much to stir up interest among a new generation of collectors. Mr. Mellon's first purchase was an album of twenty-two watercolor illustrations for the *Book of Job,* most frequently referred to in the literature as the New Zealand Set because of their having been in a private collection in that country prior to their reappearance on the market in 1928. Albin Martin (b. 1813), a pupil of Blake's most important patron in later life, the artist John Linnell (1792–1882), had taken them to New Zealand in the mid-1800s. Their authenticity has been in dispute for decades, and the consensus of scholarly opinion today is that they are the work of Linnell's circle. The execution is variable, suggesting the possibility of several hands, but at times evocative even of Linnell's best miniature technique. That Blake had no part in the production is almost certain. However, in 1941 neither Philip Hofer, the renowned curator of the Houghton Library, who actually owned the set, nor Laurence Binyon and Geoffrey Keynes, two of the greatest of Blake's scholars, who had published them in 1935 in their facsimile edition of the *Book of Job,* had any reservations whatsoever.[5] In a letter dated 17 April 1933, Binyon, who was then Keeper of Prints and Drawings at the British Museum, reassured Hofer of the sagacity of his acquisition with the observation that "the more I go into the question, the more convinced I am that your set is by Blake."[6] In the 1939 Philadelphia exhibition, Lessing J. Rosenwald's curator, Elizabeth Mongan, and Keynes's future collaborator on the 1953 Blake *Census,* Edwin Wolf 2nd, sustained that optimistic opinion. Of the rare ambivalent voices, W. Graham Robertson, whose unrivaled collection of Blake monotypes eventually went to the Tate Gallery, wrote to a fellow Blake enthusiast in the States that "the Infant's [Hofer's] 'Job' series are the rather suspicious New Zealand drawings are they not? Maybe he is well rid of them."[7]

In retrospect, the acquisition of copies, however fine their execution, may seem an inauspicious start, but Blake connoisseurship was still the monopoly of only a few scholars, and their imprimaturs had been conferred on the *Job* watercolors. At any rate, the New Zealand Set was only one of several Blake acquisitions for Mr. Mellon in 1941. Also purchased that year at the sale of Alfred Edward Newton's extensive collection was an ethereal watercolor of the *Parable of the Wise and Foolish Virgins,* a copy of the engraved *Book of Job,* and Blake's *A Descriptive Catalogue of Pictures, Poetical and Historical Inventions, Painted by William Blake* (London, 1809), which possibly belonged at one time to William Wordsworth. Another Yale notable, Wilmarth "Lefty" Lewis (whose insatiable passion for Horace Walpole culminated in the great gift to the university of the Lewis Walpole Library in Farmington), purchased at the same sale the volume of Edward Young's *The Complaint and the Consolation: or Night Thoughts* that he later presented to Paul Mellon. It was accompanied by a letter from Chauncey Tinker to Newton attesting to the authenticity of Blake's hand coloring.

But the most precursory purchase of 1941 was Copy B of Blake's first Illuminated Book, *There Is No Natural Religion,* from the heirs of William A. White.[8] From this celebrated source would ultimately derive also *Songs of Innocence* (Copy G), *Visions of the Daughters of Albion* (Copy I), and *America. A Prophecy* (Copy M). White was a legendary admirer of Shakespeare and the romantic poets, but his Blake collection, which boasted several dozen Illuminated Books and the nearly three hundred sheets of watercolor illustrations for *Night Thoughts,* was perhaps the finest and most comprehensive ever amassed. A Brooklyn native, he was a significant contributor to the development of Blake studies in America. Some of White's Blake books, including three of the Center's, came from his purchase of the library of Richard Monckton Milnes in 1903. Monckton

Milnes was the supreme Victorian dabbler—occasional poet, critic, politician, diplomat, supporter of Tennyson, friend of Swinburne and Carlyle, biographer of Keats, humorist, and speechifier—but also one of his century's most authoritative bibliophiles. Works with the covetable Monckton Milnes–White provenance abound also in the Rosenwald collection, now divided between the National Gallery and the Library of Congress.

After 1941, hardly a year passed without Mr. Mellon's acquiring some Blake opus. The harvest is impressive, consisting as it does of four tempera paintings, one monotype, several hundred prints and watercolors, and several dozen volumes with engraved illustrations; however, it is the twelve Illuminated Books that confer on this collection its stature of eminence. Between 1947 and 1949, Mr. Mellon was able to purchase Philip Hofer's copy of the *Book of Thel* (Copy B); Benjamin D'Israeli's somewhat mutilated and posthumously colored *Europe. A Prophecy* (Copy A); the copies of *Songs of Innocence* and *Songs of Experience* (Copy F) that George Cumberland (1754–1848), Blake's generous patron, had bound together in 1794; and a complete *Songs of Innocence and of Experience* (Copy L) that has no known marvelous pedigree despite its quiet excellence. In the 1950s the three previously cited titles from the White collection were added, as were a second copy of the *Book of Thel* (Copy R) and one of the few copies of *The [First] Book of Urizen* (Copy A) with a full complement of twenty-eight plates. The final Illuminated Book to enter the collection, in 1972, was a second copy, quite differently colored, of *Urizen* (Copy C), thus bringing together two of only eight known printings of that magnificent prophetic work.

In assessing this achievement, one should recall that in 1941 Paul Mellon was the cadet member of a distinguished group of bibliophiles who had made it their business to transfer the great Blake collections from private to public ownership—in particular, Henry E. Huntington, Lessing J. Rosenwald, and Mrs. Landon K. Thorne in America, and W. Graham Robertson and Sir Geoffrey Keynes in England. But where the Mellon collection may want the depth or the comprehensiveness of these other major cumulations, it ultimately ranks with them primarily because of two stellar acquisitions: the one hundred sixteen watercolor illustrations for the poems of Thomas Gray, and the most coveted of Blake's composite art of poetry, painting, and printmaking, the unique, colored copy of *Jerusalem* (Copy E).

Jerusalem. The Emanation of the Giant Albion—that "tremendous piece of ordnance," as the artist T. G. Wainewright (1794–1852) aptly described his own copy—occupied Blake from 1804, the date inscribed on the title page, until the last years of his life.[9] Recently it has stimulated considerable discussion, with various authors tracing its genesis or plumbing its great obscurity with an enthusiasm equal to the formidable task. Blake informed his readers on plate 38 that it was during his sojourn with Hayley at Felpham (1800–1803) that "I heard and saw the vision of Albion." He had, in fact, written to his patron Thomas Butts (1759–1845) in April 1803 that "none can know the Spiritual Acts of my three years' Slumber on the banks of the Ocean [Felpham], unless he has seen them in the spirit, or unless he should read my long poem descriptive of these Acts; for I have in these three years composed an immense number of verses on One Grand Theme, Similar to Homer's Iliad or Milton's Paradise Lost, the Persons and Machinery entirely new to the Inhabitants of Earth."[10] *Jerusalem* was part of this epic story of spiritual redemption in which all opposing forces within man are reconciled in the eternal unity of Christ's sacrifice. The poem was certainly not completed at Felpham, and it would stand many revisions over the years, but it must have been sufficiently advanced for Blake to commence production of the plates after renouncing Hayley's intrusive patronage in 1803. By 1807 there existed sixty etched plates, according to George Cumberland.[11] Two years later, Blake referred to the work in his *Descriptive Catalogue* as having been composed "under inspiration. . . . It is voluminous, and contains the ancient history of Britain, and the world of Satan and Adam,"[12] and in 1812 he exhibited at the annual exhibition of the Associated Painters in Watercolours "Detached Specimens" from among the finished plates. These were probably similar to several proof impressions now in the Mellon collection. It would appear, however, that the project was, and perhaps could only have been, brought to fruition after John Linnell entered Blake's life in 1818. Of the five complete copies of *Jerusalem* printed during Blake's lifetime, the first was purchased by Linnell in 1819 and another by the artist William Young Ottley (1771–1836), through the agency of Linnell, on the eve of Blake's death.[13]

With the exception of the Mellon copy, which the artist printed in about 1821 in orange-red ink and, by his standards, lavishly hand colored, the remaining copies are monochromatic. Printed in black, they offer a visual density much closer to that of a conventional printed book and, in all likelihood, intentional allusions to medieval woodcuts. But they lack both the enchanting lyricism of the delicately washed pages of unadorned text in the Mellon copy and the majesty and narrative interest that Blake's coloring imparts to certain formal elements in its illustrations. The labor involved in printing its one hundred plates, not to mention the time required to finish them fastidiously with watercolors, touches of gold paint, and numerous strokes of the pen, argued against any deluxe edition of this masterwork. In a letter to Cumberland of 12 April 1827, a few months before his death, Blake seemed resigned to these restraints on his illusion of securing material satisfaction from his efforts: "I have been near the Gates of Death and have returned very weak and an Old Man feeble and tottering, but not in Spirit and Life, not in the Real Man, the Imagination which Livith for Ever. . . . The Last work I produced is a Poem Entitled Jerusalem the Emanation of the Giant Albion, but find that to print it will cost my time the amount of Twenty Guineas [one year]. One I have finished. It contains 100 plates but it is not likely that I shall get a Customer for it."[14] This single "finished" copy to which Blake refers is unquestionably Yale's. As he had predicted, it remained unsold and passed, with the death of Catherine Blake, to her executor Frederick Tatham. Tatham found most of Blake's poetry unintelligible and *Jerusalem* "not only abstruse but according to common rules of criticism as near ridiculous, as it is heterogeneous."[15] He nevertheless admired the industry and graphics of *Jerusalem* sufficiently to have three copies printed from the copper plates he had inherited and to pen a twenty-four-page biography of Blake as a preface to the Mellon copy, in which he allowed, not without justifiable confidence, that "the designs are possessed of . . . some of the most noble conceptions possible to the mind of man. You may doubt however the means and you may criticise the peculiarity of the notions, but . . . Michel Angelo, Julio Romano or any other great man never surpassed plates 25, 35, 37, 46, 51, 76, 94 and many of the stupendous and awful scenes with which this laborious work is so thickly ornamented."[16]

Tatham probably sold Copy E to George Blamire (1788–1863), a distant relation of the poet Susannah Blamire, also known as the Muse of Cumberland. Although an affluent barrister with large estates in that county, Blamire surprisingly occupied only three rooms on the first floor of a London townhouse and is said to have slept in his armchair the last sixteen years of his life. His modest accommodations, barely more commodious than Blake's two small rooms in Fountain Court, were nevertheless superbly appointed in that they also housed two of Mr. Mellon's finest tempera paintings, *The Horse* and *The Virgin and Child,* or the *"Black Madonna."* Mr. Mellon purchased *Jerusalem* in 1953 from the collection formed by Sir William Stirling-Maxwell at the end of the nineteenth century. From the same source and in the same year, he acquired, and immediately donated to the Victoria and Albert Museum, the rather hard-edged tempera of *The Virgin and Child in Egypt* (1810).[17] This was not his first Blake donation to a public institution. In 1949 he and Mrs. Thorne had made possible the purchase by the Morgan Library of twelve watercolor illustrations for Milton's *L'Allegro* and *Il Penseroso*.[18]

We may never know why Blake produced such an elaborate copy of *Jerusalem* without any obvious client on hand to remunerate him, or why he seems to have priced the work beyond the interest of even his most munificent patrons, like Butts. Perhaps he simply meant, in the end, to keep it for himself as an exemplar. It is, after all, the consummation of his genius as a poet, artist, and prophetic revolutionary, his longest and most personal testament of beliefs, his most brilliantly designed and technically innovative work of art.

No such uncertainty exists as to the commission and destination of the watercolor illustrations for Thomas Gray's *Poems*. The years between 1790 and 1805 were the most fecund of Blake's career, although external circumstances relentlessly threatened his solvency. The wars with France and the collapse of the international print trade occasioned hardships throughout the London art world, but especially for reproductive engravers. Since Blake's Illuminated Books, of which fewer than two hundred copies were ever sold in his lifetime, appealed to a finite audience, the artist welcomed, albeit with faltering compliance, sporadic commissions of mechanical engraving from commercial publishers like Joseph Johnson, Richard Edwards, or the much-reviled Robert Cromek. "I curse and bless Engraving alternately, because it takes so much time and is intractable, tho' capable of such beauty and perfection," he wrote to William Hayley in 1804.[19] But more important to his modest sustenance and spiritual composure was the generosity of friends, among whom the sculptor John Flaxman occupied an esteemed position. In 1783, Flaxman helped subsidize the publication of Blake's first poems, *Poetical Sketches,* and he later introduced the artist to Hayley and other patrons. More to the point, Flaxman's wife, Ann, known more familiarly as Nancy, wrote in 1797 that her husband had employed Blake to "illuminate the works of Gray for my library" as a birthday present.[20] The commencement of this project followed immediately the conclusion of Richard Edwards's grandiose commission of five hundred watercolors and forty-three engraved designs for Edward Young's *Night Thoughts*. As with that scheme,

Blake adopted for Gray the novel format of surrounding an existing page of letterpress with a much larger watercolor and pen design. Analogies to this type of presentation appear in the Illuminated Books, but especially in the most complex of the later *Jerusalem* designs.

Blake had no reservations illustrating another poet's work; rather, he treated Gray's verse, as he had Young's, as a stimulus for his own imaginative flights. A full range of sentiments coax the reader through the leaves of this remarkable manuscript. More often than not, Blake's designs are replete with the fine madness, the allusions and inventions of whimsical genius that, while wondrous to us and delightful, no doubt, to Nancy and John Flaxman, might well have discomfited the more stately Gray. Design 28 of *The Long Story,* for instance, in which the appearance of the Wizard Poet scatters terrified children and farmyard animals, is a jaunty reprise of Rembrandt's etched *Annunciation to the Shepherds*.

If *Elegy Written in a Country Church-Yard* was Gray's most famous poem—"one of the most classical productions ever penned by a refined and thoughtful mind moralizing on human life"[21]—its stature was not evident in Blake's treatment. He was more fascinated by and responsive to *The Bard*. He illustrated Gray's pindaric ode in different media beginning as early as 1785. That he fancied himself a modern incarnation of this mythical Welsh poet is presumed, and the ode inevitably inspired the most monumental and heroic of his designs for Mrs. Flaxman. *The Bard "Weaving the Winding Sheet of Edward's Race"* is a riveting example of imaginative elucidation. The loom of Edward I's fate is envisioned as a harp of huge strings weeping blood droplets, on which the Bard chants his augury of the king's demise.

John Flaxman survived his wife by six years, and at the sale of their collection in 1828 the Gray watercolors passed to William Beckford (1760–1844) of Fonthill Abbey, that sublime eccentric who already owned a respectable group of Blake's books. His daughter, the Duchess of Hamilton, inherited the *Gray* in 1844, after which the drawings remained, virtually unknown and unstudied, in the possession of the Dukes of Hamilton until purchased by Paul Mellon in 1966. Prior to that date, in March 1949, Geoffrey Keynes and others had founded The William Blake Trust to promote the continued study of the poet through the publication of accurate color reproductions of his greatest works. The unique Copy E of *Jerusalem,* which had not yet entered the Mellon collection, was the first major project undertaken for the Trust by Arnold Fawcus, director of the Trianon Press in Paris. In 1962, Mr. Mellon was elected an associate trustee, and from 1966 to 1970 he supported financially, and with matchless patience, the exacting production of the jewel of the Trust's collotype and stencil replications, *William Blake's Water-Colour Designs for the Poems of Thomas Gray* (1971). This was merely one of many instances of Paul Mellon's commitment to the programs of the Blake Trust.

While negotiating the sale of the Gray watercolors, the distinguished bibliophile John Carter, of Sotheby's, wrote to Mellon, "You, as I know from our Stirling-*Jerusalem* deal of a dozen years ago, are primarily interested in Blake's illustrated *books*, rather than in his easel pictures. This *is* an illustrated *book*." Carter was only partially correct in his assessment of Mr. Mellon's interests. Certainly the Illuminated Books had been the object of the hunt in the 1940s and 1950s, but in 1961 Mr. Mellon had seriously broadened the scope of his collection with the acquisition of four tempera paintings. Blake used some form of water-based pigments in the production of preparatory sketches and finished works of art from the beginning of his career. In the 1790s transparent watercolor was his medium of choice for the often prodigious series of illustrations he made to his own and other poets' works. But in 1799, Thomas Butts, a clerk in the office of the Commissary General of Musters, commissioned fifty easel paintings of biblical subjects, which Blake promised to execute in a medium he described initially as tempera and later as fresco. His great aversion to the indistinctness of oil painting is documented throughout his writings on art, hence his experiments with alternative media. Blake's improvised "fresco" medium has proved unstable with time, but in its original state it would have imbued his pictures with an opalescence and a clarity that he found wanting in oil painting. *Abraham and Isaac* and *Christ Giving Sight to Bartimaeus* are two of the Butts temperas that have come to Yale. After 1800, Blake seems to have preferred the limpidity of pure watercolor in continuing his work for Butts. That would include another one hundred biblical illustrations, of which the remarkably well-preserved *Mary Magdalen at the Sepulchre* is a splendid contrivance of gothic symmetry and a masterful display of Blake's command of watercolor.

Another tempera that Mr. Mellon acquired at this time, *The Horse,* is decidedly not an easel picture and was probably not intended for Butts but is indisputably the gem of the painting collection. Identical in size to the small engraved illustration for Hayley's *Ballads* (1805) that it reproduces, it might be one of the "little high finished Pictures the size the Engravings are to be" mentioned by Blake in a letter to Hayley of March 1805.[22] If so, it is the only surviving example, but the many similarities between *The Horse* and the intricately rendered and richly textured large color prints of 1805, irrespective of their different media, certainly justify this supposition.

Butts, Flaxman, and Hayley, not to mention other friends like Cumberland and Henry Fuseli (1741–1825), who purchased as a present in 1806 the Center's copy of *For Children: The Gates of Paradise* (Copy E), were liberal and constant in their support of the Blakes. Nevertheless, following the publication in 1808 of Robert Blair's *The Grave,* for which Blake designed the illustrations but was denied the satisfaction of engraving them by a publisher fearful of his unorthodox printmaking inventions, the artist practically disappeared from public view until rediscovered and lionized by John Linnell in the late teens. In fact, he was actually declared dead by a publisher who, in appropriating one of his engraved *Night Thoughts* designs for service as a frontispiece to *The Seraph, a Collection of Sacred Music* (1818), had the reengraved plate inscribed "Drawn by the late W. Blake Esq. RA."

Several objects in the Mellon collection hint at what Blake was about during those years of obscurity. A stock but interesting assignment, in light of the artist's love of the antique, was the delicate graphite study of the *Laocoön* he later engraved to illustrate an article on sculpture that Flaxman had written for Rees's *Cyclopaedia*. According to Frederick Tatham's inscription across the bottom of the sheet, when Blake was making this study among the students in the cast room of the Royal Academy in 1815, Fuseli arrived and announced, "Why Mr. Blake. You a student. You ought to teach us." Indeed, Blake was engaged in some informal teaching during this period, and he was probably a more familiar habitué of the Royal Academy than can be documented. The engraver Seymour Kirkup (1788–1880) recalled, in a letter to Monckton Milnes, that he had been "much with Blake from 1810 to 1816" when he was a student in the antique school. Although he thought Blake mad at the time, he later regretted not having valued his "high qualities" and "honest manner."[23]

Another student working at the Royal Academy during this period was the engraver William Ensom (1796–1832), the likely first owner of one of the Center's copies of Young's *Night Thoughts*, which he inscribed "coloured for me by Mr. Blake." Gerald Bentley Jr. has recorded twenty-six colored copies of Young, but Catherine Blake was probably responsible for most of this handiwork, including the present example.[24] Ensom is best remembered as a friend of the painter Richard Parkes Bonington (1802–1828), but prior to moving to Paris in about 1818 he appears to have passed an apprenticeship under Charles Warren (d. 1823), engraver to the Bank of England. He was awarded, in 1815, a silver medal by the Society of Arts for a pen and ink portrait of Blake. Unfortunately, the circumstances that occasioned that portrait, and the portrait itself, are now unknown. William Haines (1778–1848), an engraver and miniature painter with whom Blake had collaborated on the plates to Hayley's *Life of Romney* (1809), also emerged as a patron during this period. Haines is the earliest recorded owner of *The Parable of the Wise and Foolish Virgins,* a more atmospheric version of a watercolor composition painted for Butts in 1805. John Linnell and Sir Thomas Lawrence (1769–1830), president of the Royal Academy, also commissioned versions of this popular invention in the 1820s.

Blake had trained for seven years as a reproductive engraver, and he practiced that trade his entire career, revising his style with ingenuity as the commissions or his own predilection dictated. Mr. Mellon was no less attentive to this dimension of Blake's oeuvre than to any other. How varied are Blake's approaches, as demonstrated by random examples in the Center's printroom—from the expressive scratchiness of the emblematic *For Children* to the polished professionalism of the *Portrait of Lavater* to the classical linearity of the *Night Thoughts* designs to the archaism of the great *Chaucer's Canterbury Pilgrims*. He was equally comfortable with new or experimental techniques of his own or of another's creation, such as his relief etchings and the large monotypes he produced in multiple sets between 1795 and 1805, including the Center's Shakespeare illustration *Pity*. The popular technique of lithography entered his repertoire in the 1820s, and he assayed wood engraving only once, but with seductive originality. All of these fascinate, but the *Illustrations of the Book of Job,* commissioned by Linnell in 1823, stand apart as a tour-de-force of the engraver's art, intentionally evocative of early Northern engraving yet thoroughly modern in their delicately crafted brilliance. They are a paean to an underrated art, and only the most accomplished of Turner's troop of reproductive engravers, buoyed by his personal sensibility and regimented by his colossal creative stewardship, could approach Blake's mastery of the burin. The Center is fortunate to claim two *Job* portfolios, as they go a long way in compensating for the disappointment of the New Zealand Set of watercolor copies.

In 1979, Mr. Mellon made his last Blake purchase to date: *The Man Sweeping the Interpreter's Parlour,* of c. 1822. It is, coincidentally, also one of Blake's last engravings. Possibly another Linnell commission, its technique has actually eluded definitive identification, resembling both the wood engravings for Thornton's *The Pastorals of Virgil* (1821) and the inky, relief-etched plate 51 of *Jerusalem*.[25] The antinomian subject is a passage from Bunyan's *Pilgrim's Progress,* in which an old man reminiscent of Urizen and representing moral law stirs up the dust of corruption in the soul of a man as an angel attempts to calm the clouds, billowing with Goyaesque demons, by sprinkling the floor with the cleansing grace of the Gospel. We alight once again on Blake's favorite theme—redemption—borrowed from another author and recast with simplicity in the visual language of his own mythology, a succinct and graceful complement to the elaborate apparatus of *Jerusalem*.

By visiting the British Art Center it is certainly possible to gain an overview of the accomplishments of a number of artists who were profoundly gifted or whose contributions proved seminal to the development of the art of their epoch. Exceptional groups of oils, drawings, and prints—by Turner, Gainsborough, Hogarth, and Stubbs, to name but a few artists—elicit admiration for the national school and the individual celebrities it produced. But William Blake invariably commands a different respect, for although most of his contemporaries were accomplished in several media and some even dabbled in writing verse or composing music, none have produced a body of work quite as fabulous in its meaning and intriguingly unorthodox in its means as Blake's. In the course of preparing this text, I was emboldened to read *Jerusalem* once again; not the published critical edition nor either of the two splendid facsimiles by the Blake Trust but the original Copy E. It is a potent experience that all visitors to the Study Room of the British Art Center have license to share; and until one has, it is impossible to grasp the manifold genius of its creator, or the special order of Paul Mellon's philanthropy.

This book and its accompanying special exhibition commemorate the twentieth anniversary of the opening of the Yale Center for British Art in 1977. The appropriateness of the enterprise needs no illumination. It is customary to dedicate such a volume, but the artworks it describes are the truly legitimate testament to Paul Mellon, who has prized their literary and artistic value and assured that generations of sympathetic minds will enjoy unencumbered access to them. Our collective obligation to him is great, as is my personal debt of gratitude for the pleasure these collections have afforded me over the years. My prefatory remarks have relied largely on Mr. Mellon's autobiography and other published accounts of his progress as a collector and bibliophile over sixty years. I have also benefited from the able assistance of Beverly Carter in Virginia, Joseph Viscomi in Chapel Hill, and Susan Greenberg in New Haven. Any omissions or inaccuracies are mine alone. Finally, the staff of the museum and our colleagues at Yale University Press have responded, as always, with timely professionalism.

NOTES

1. I am grateful to David Bindman (letter, 1996) for confirming my attribution of this previously unrecorded work.

2. Blake began collecting prints by Dürer and other sixteenth-century masters as early as his apprenticeship years; see Benjamin Heath Malkin, *A Father's Memoirs of His Child* (London, 1806), xix.

3. Paul Mellon, *Reflections in a Silver Spoon: A Memoir* (New York, 1992), 293.

4. Ibid., 284.

5. See Laurence Binyon and Geoffrey Keynes, *Illustrations of the Book of Job by William Blake* (New York, 1935).

6. The letter accompanied the watercolors and is now at the Yale Center for British Art.

7. *Letters to Frances White Emerson from W. Graham Robertson* (n.p., 1948), 56.

8. The convention of identifying individual copies of the Illuminated Books with letters was established in Geoffrey Keynes and Edwin Wolf 2nd, *William Blake's Illuminated Books: A Census* (New York, 1953).

9. See Wainewright's letter of September 1820 to *The London Magazine,* reprinted in G. E. Bentley Jr., *Blake Records* (Oxford, 1969), 265–66.

10. Geoffrey Keynes, Kt., *The Letters of William Blake* (Oxford, 1980), 55.

11. As recorded in Cumberland's notebook; see Bentley, *Records,* 187.

12. *A Descriptive Catalogue of Pictures, Poetical and Historical Inventions, Painted by William Blake* (London, 1809), 42. This publication accompanied Blake's private exhibition of his works.

13. There is no mention of *Jerusalem* in the list of prices for printing his books that Blake sent the antiquary Dawson Turner on 9 June 1818 (Keynes, *Letters,* 133), suggesting that either he was unwilling to print a copy of *Jerusalem* for Turner or he had not yet finished it. Most scholars accept the latter hypothesis.

14. Keynes, *Letters,* 168–69.

15. Frederick Tatham, *Life of Blake,* 10. This manuscript is in the Yale Center for British Art.

16. Ibid., 10.

17. Martin Butlin, *The Paintings and Drawings of William Blake*, 2 vols. (New Haven, 1981), no. 669.

18. Ibid., no. 543.

19. Keynes, *Letters,* 63.

20. See Mary Woodworth, "Blake's Illustrations to Gray," *Notes and Queries,* 215 (1970): 312–13.

21. William Hazlitt, "Lecture VI: On Swift, Young, Gray, Collins etc.," in *Lectures on the English Poets,* 3rd ed. (London, 1859), 140.

22. Keynes, *Letters,* 111.

23. T. Wemyss Reid, *The Life, Letters, and Friendships of Richard Monckton Milnes, First Lord Houghton,* 3rd ed. (London, 1891), 2:222.

24. G. E. Bentley Jr., *Blake Books Supplement* (Oxford, 1995), 269ff. According to Tatham, *Life of Blake,* 22: "She even laboured upon his works, those parts of them where powers of drawing & form were not necessary, which from her excellent Idea of Colouring, was of no small use in the completion of his laborious designs. This she did to a much greater extent than is usually credited." Many of these copies were colored by the same hand and in the same manner. In conventional printshop practice of the period, Catherine Blake would have worked from one model colored by the artist.

25. For the most complete discussion of this problem, see Robert N. Essick, *The Separate Plates of William Blake: A Catalogue* (Princeton, 1983), 110. His argument that the design was engraved in relief on a metal plate is probably the most accurate.

CHRONOLOGY OF THE LIFE OF WILLIAM BLAKE

1757   "I believe it has been invariably the custom of every age, whenever a man has been found to depart from the usual mode of thinking, to consider him of deranged intellect, and not unfrequently stark staring mad. . . . Bearing this stigma of eccentricity, William Blake, with most extraordinary zeal, commenced his efforts in art under the roof of no. 28 Broad Street, in which house he was born, and where his father carried on the business of a hosier."—John Thomas Smith, *Nollekens and His Times,* London, 1829

1767/68   Blake entered Henry Pars's drawing academy in the Strand.

1771–1779   The antiquarian engraver James Basire (1730–1802) took Blake as his apprentice for seven years. He probably lived with Basire at 31 Great Queen Street, Lincoln's Inn Fields.

1773   First known engraving, after a figure in Michelangelo's *Crucifixion of St. Peter.* Blake later dated the work when he reengraved the plate as *Joseph of Arimathea among the Rocks of Albion.*

1774/75   Earliest attributable drawings of monuments in Westminster Abbey. These Blake later engraved for Richard Gough's *Sepulchral Monuments in Great Britain* (1786).

1779   Enrolled as an engraver at the Royal Academy Schools, where he formed long-standing friendships with fellow students John Flaxman (1756–1826) and Thomas Stothard (1755–1834).

1780   First exhibit at the Royal Academy: a watercolor titled *The Death of Earl Godwin.*

1782   Robert Blake (probably born 1767), Blake's youngest and favorite brother, is also enrolled as an engraver at the Royal Academy Schools. In August, Blake married Catherine Butcher (or Boucher, born 25 April 1762) and moved to 23 Green Street, Leicester Fields.

1783   Publication of *Poetical Sketches* financed by John Flaxman and the Rev. and Mrs. A. S. Matthew.

1784   In July, Blake's father died, leaving him a small inheritance, which he used to set himself up as a print seller and publisher with James Parker (1750–1805), a friend from the Basire shop. Their two stipple engravings after Stothard's *Zephyrus and Flora* and *Callisto* are the principal surviving evidence of this partnership.

1785   Exhibited four watercolors at the Royal Academy, including an illustration for Thomas Gray's *The Bard.*

1787   The death of Robert Blake precipitated an emotional crisis.

1787/88   Befriended the painter Henry Fuseli (1741–1825). According to Frederick Tatham (1805–1878), whose manuscript *Life of Blake* was written to accompany the only complete hand-colored copy of *Jerusalem* (both now at Yale), "Blake was more fond of Fuseli than any other man on earth."

1788	Experimented with relief printing techniques in *There Is No Natural Religion* and *All Religions Are One*. Sympathetic to the ideals of the American and French revolutions, Blake began associating with the radical circle of Mary Wollstonecraft, William Godwin, Joseph Priestly, Thomas Paine, and Joseph Johnson, "the bookseller of St. Paul's Churchyard."
1789/90	The twelve illustrations for *Tiriel*, Blake's first prophetic manuscript (British Library) were probably designed at this time. *Songs of Innocence* and *The Book of Thel* were issued. In April, Blake and his wife signed articles of belief at the first general conference of the Swedenborgian New Jerusalem Church but never actually became members. The next year Blake began *The Marriage of Heaven and Hell*, a satirical assault upon Swedenborg and the institutionalization of the New Church.
1791	Johnson published Blake's illustrations for Mary Wollstonecraft's *Original Stories from Real Life*.
1793	*Visions of the Daughters of Albion; America. A Prophecy;* and the first version of *For Children: The Gates of Paradise* issued.
1794	*Songs of Experience; Europe. A Prophecy;* and *The [First] Book of Urizen* issued.
1795	*The Song of Los; The Book of Ahania;* and *The Book of Los* completed. Richard Edwards commissioned the illustrations for Edward Young's *Night Thoughts* (published 1797).
1796	George Cumberland (1754–1848) included eight Blake engravings in his *Thoughts on Outline*. The artist probably began the unfinished manuscript *Vala*, or *The Four Zoas*.
1797	Commissioned by John Flaxman to illustrate, as a present for his wife, Ann, an edition of Thomas Gray's *Poems*. The 116 watercolor designs are now at Yale.
1799	Began work on what would become an exhaustive series of biblical illustrations for a new patron, Thomas Butts (1759–1845).
1800	Three engravings by Blake after Flaxman appear in William Hayley's *Essay on Sculpture*. In September, Blake moved to Hayley's home at Felpham, where he was employed as an engraver, decorative artist, and miniature painter.
1801	Flaxman introduced Blake to another patron, the Rev. Joseph Thomas, who commissioned watercolor illustrations for Milton's *Comus*. He also received a commission to produce an engraving for Fuseli's *Lectures on Painting*.
1802	First series of Hayley's *Ballads* published in installments, with engravings by Blake.
1803	Six engravings by Blake published in Hayley's *Life of Cowper*. Six plates after Maria Flaxman (the sculptor's sister-in-law) embellish Hayley's *Triumphs of Temper*. A confrontation with a soldier named John Scolfield led to charges of sedition, of which Blake was later acquitted. The plates for Hayley's *Life of George Romney* were begun, but in September Blake left Felpham and returned to London.
1804	The plates for *Milton. A Poem* and *Jerusalem* begun.
1805	Hayley's *Ballads* reissued with five engravings by Blake. The artist resumed his biblical watercolors for Butts, including his first series of illustrations for the *Book of Job*. He was also commissioned by Robert Hartley Cromek to illustrate and engrave a deluxe edition of Robert Blair's *The Grave;* however, on

	seeing Blake's proof of *Death's Door,* Cromek transferred the engraving commission to Luigi Schiavonetti.
1806	An engraving by Cromek after Blake used as the frontispiece for Benjamin Heath Malkin's *A Father's Memoirs of His Child,* which included the earliest biographical notice of Blake.
1807	George Cumberland recorded that Blake had finished sixty of the *Jerusalem* etchings by this year.
1808	*The Grave* was published with twelve etchings by Schiavonetti after Blake and a frontispiece after Thomas Phillips's oil portrait of Blake. The artist executed the second, and finest, set of watercolor illustrations for Milton's *Paradise Lost.*
1809	*A Descriptive Catalogue* accompanied Blake's private exhibition, which focused on his tempera paintings. It opened in May at his brother's house, 28 Broad Street, and continued well into 1810.
1810	Completed engraving *Chaucer's Canterbury Pilgrims.* Blake had considered producing a large engraving of this subject for commercial distribution as early as 1806. Stothard, under the auspices of Cromek, produced a similar print, thereby alienating Blake, who accused both publisher and artist of appropriating his idea.
1812	Four works exhibited with the Associated Painters in Watercolours, including "Detached Specimens of an original illuminated poem entitled *Jerusalem.*"
1815	Engraved a plate of the *Laocoön,* based on his drawing at Yale, taken from a cast in the Royal Academy. The engraving was published in Rees's *Cyclopedia* (1820). Blake contracted by the Wedgwood firm to engrave pattern-book designs.
1816	*L'Allegro* and *Il Penseroso* watercolors and the second series of *Comus* illustrations executed for Butts.
1818	Blake met John Linnell (1792–1882), who became his chief supporter and patron in his last years. Through Linnell he met John Varley (1778–1842) and John Constable (1775–1837). *For Children: The Gates of Paradise* (1793) was revised and reissued as *For the Sexes: The Gates of Paradise.* Coleridge, after reading a copy of *Songs,* made his famous remark that Blake "is a man of Genius—and I apprehend, a Swedenborgian—Certainly, a mystic *emphatically.*"
1819	At Varley's insistence, Blake began drawing "visionary heads." Through Linnell, an introduction to Dr. Robert John Thornton resulted in a commission to illustrate Virgil.
1821	The *Pastorals of Virgil* were published with seventeen of Blake's wood engravings. His financial position deteriorating, the artist was forced to sell his print collection at Colnaghi's and to accept a charity from the Royal Academy. Moved to 3 Fountain Court, Strand.
1822	*The Ghost of Abel* was printed. Probable date of *On Homer's Poetry and On Virgil.*
1823	Linnell commissioned the engraved *Illustrations of the Book of Job* (published 1826).
1824	Samuel Palmer (1805–1881) probably made Blake's acquaintance. Linnell commissioned illustrations to Dante, of which 102 watercolors and 7 engravings were completed before Blake's death.
1825	Blake met George Richmond (1809–1896), Edward Calvert (1799–1833), Francis

	Oliver Finch (1802–1862), and other artists who considered themselves his adherents.
1827	On 12 August, Blake died at his home at 3 Fountain Court. His widow, Catherine, was taken in first by Linnell and then, until her death in 1831, by Frederick Tatham. "He made a drawing [of Catherine], which though not a likeness is finely touched and expressed. He then threw that down, after having drawn for an hour and began to sing Hallelujahs and songs of joy and triumph which Mrs. Blake described as being truly sublime in music and in verse. . . . Such was the entertainment of the last hour of his life. His bursts of gladness made the room peal again. The walls rang and resounded with the beatific vision. It was the prelude to the hymns of saints. It was an overture to the choir of heaven. It was a chant for the response of angels."—Tatham, *Life of Blake*.

PLATES

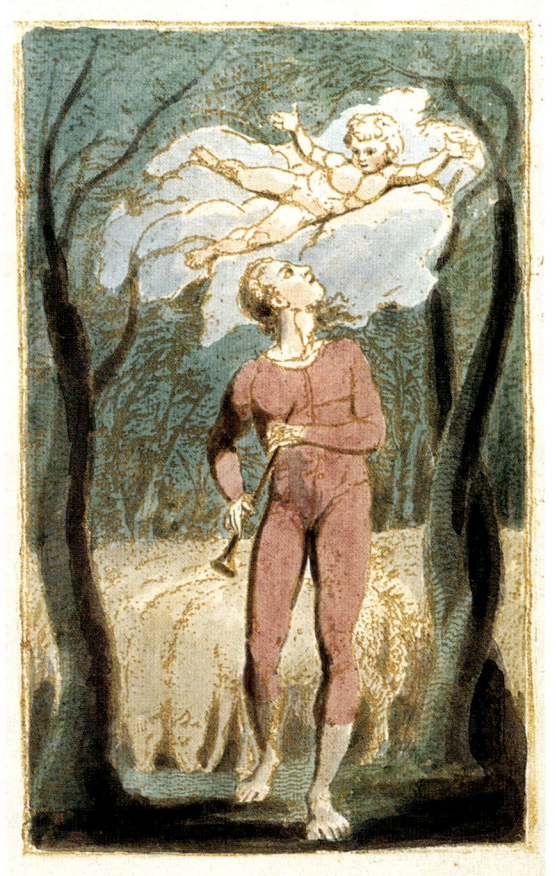
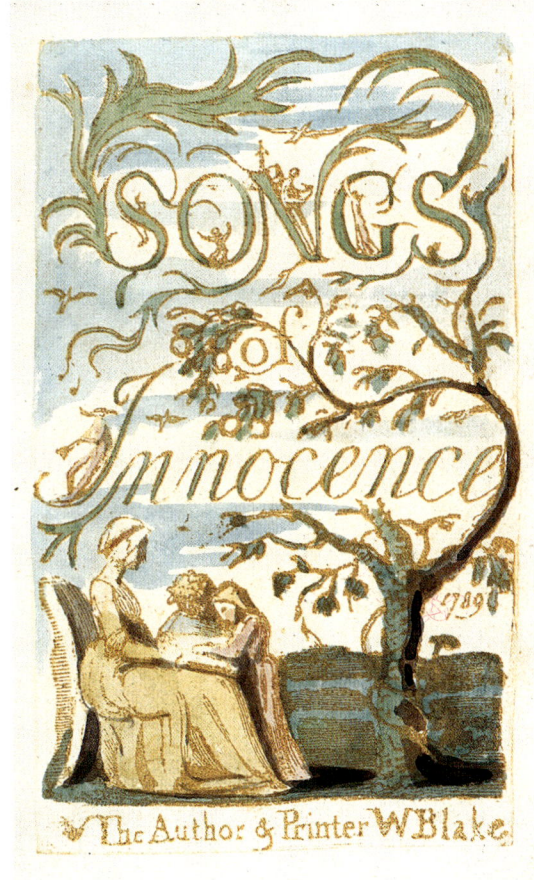

Songs of Innocence, Copy G, frontispiece,
relief etching with pen and ink and watercolor

Songs of Innocence, Copy G, title page,
relief etching with pen and ink and watercolor

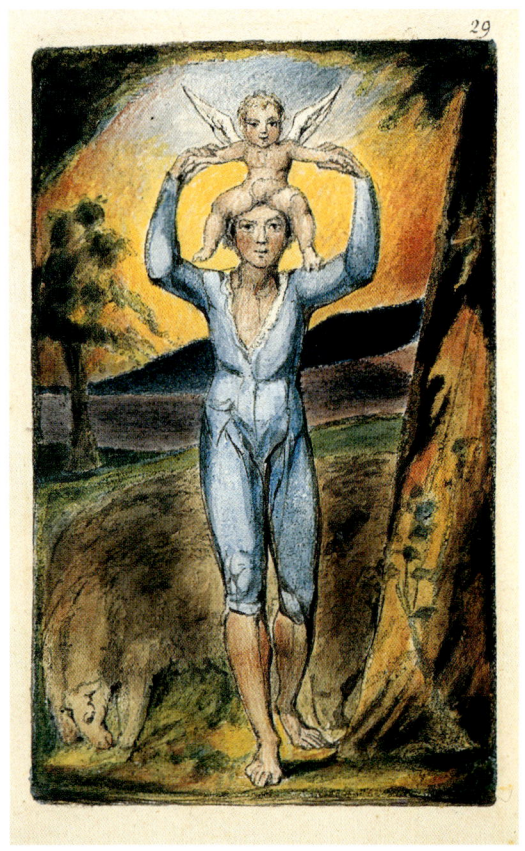
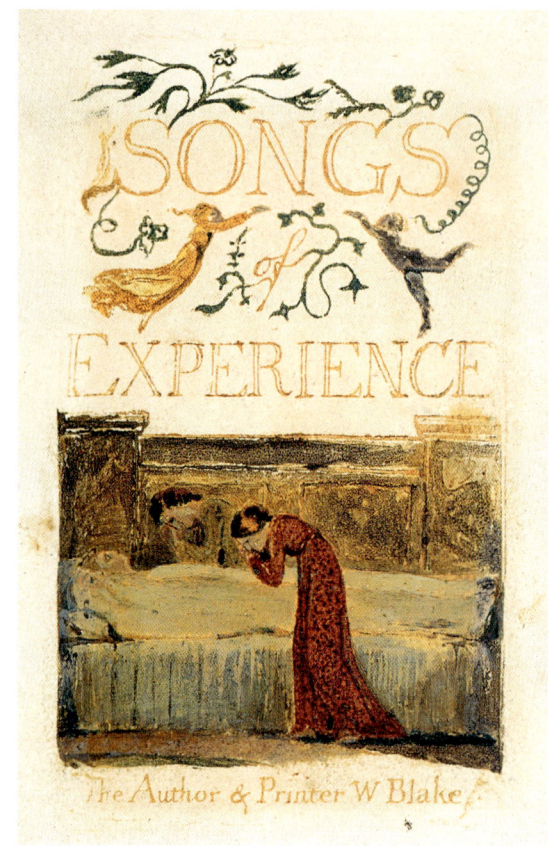

Songs of Innocence and of Experience, Copy L,
Experience frontispiece,
relief etching with pen and ink and watercolor

Songs of Experience, Copy F, title page,
color-printed relief etching with watercolor

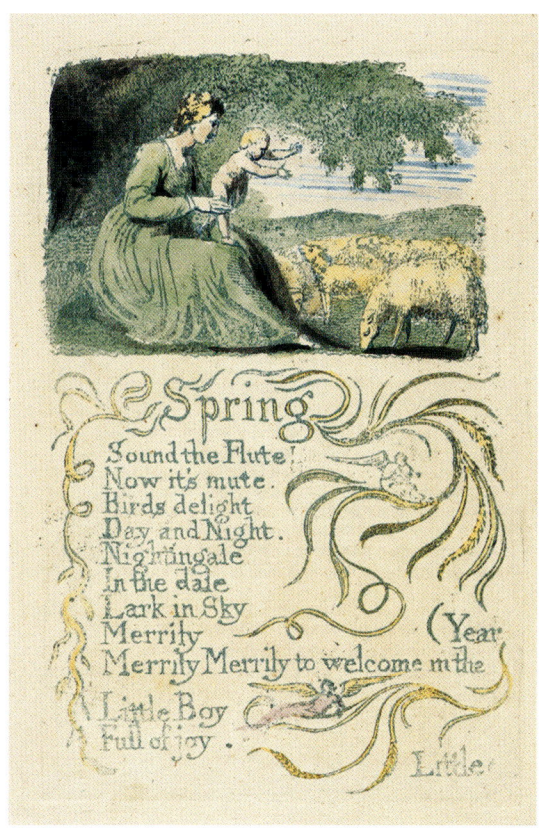

Songs of Innocence, Copy F, pl. 10,
Spring, relief etching with watercolor

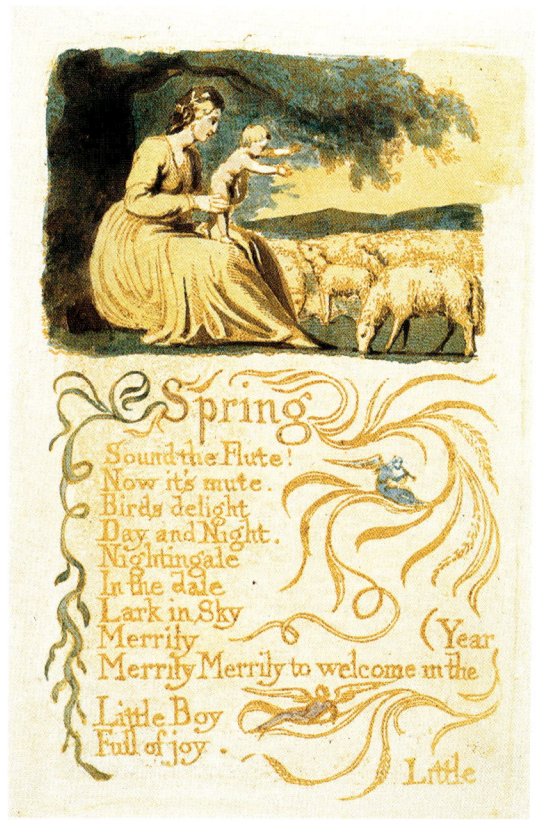

Songs of Innocence, Copy G, pl. 25,
Spring, relief etching with watercolor

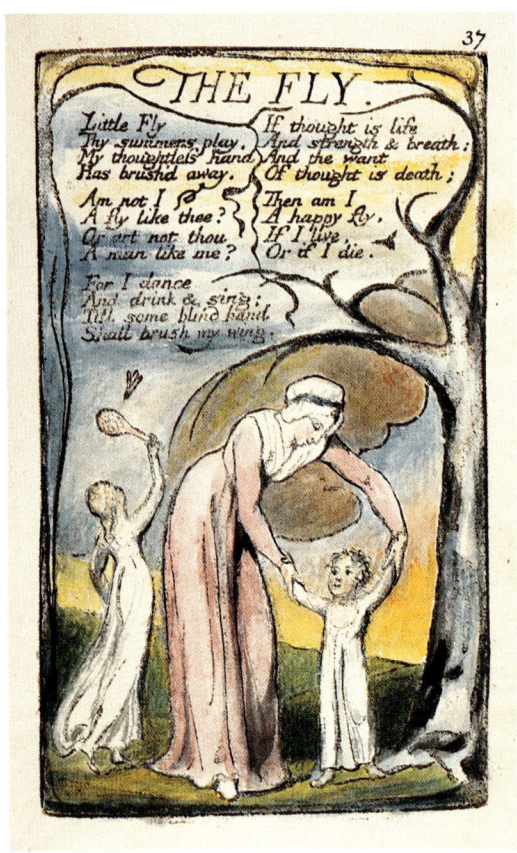
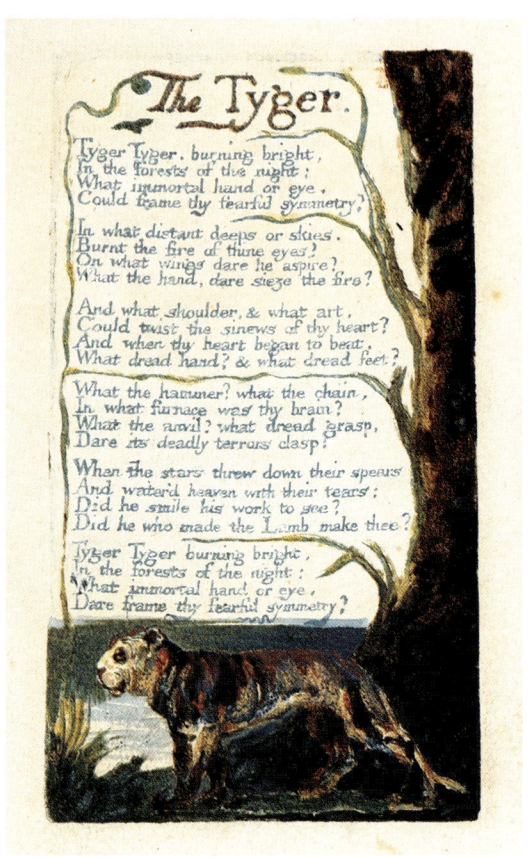

Songs of Innocence and of Experience, Copy L, pl. 37, *The Fly,* relief etching with pen and ink and watercolor

Songs of Experience, Copy F, pl. 41, *The Tyger,* color-printed relief etching with watercolor

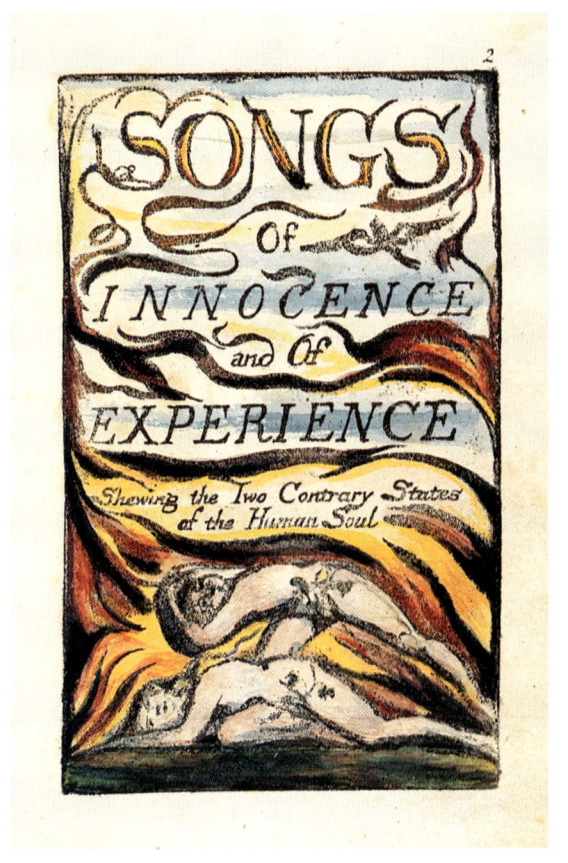
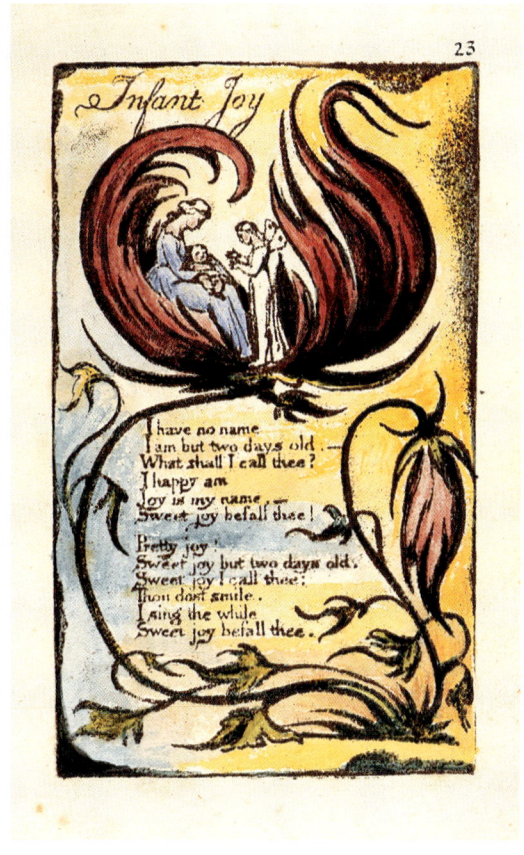

Songs of Innocence and of Experience, Copy L, Combined title page, relief etching with pen and ink and watercolor

Songs of Innocence and of Experience, Copy L, pl. 23, *Infant Joy,* relief etching with pen and ink and watercolor

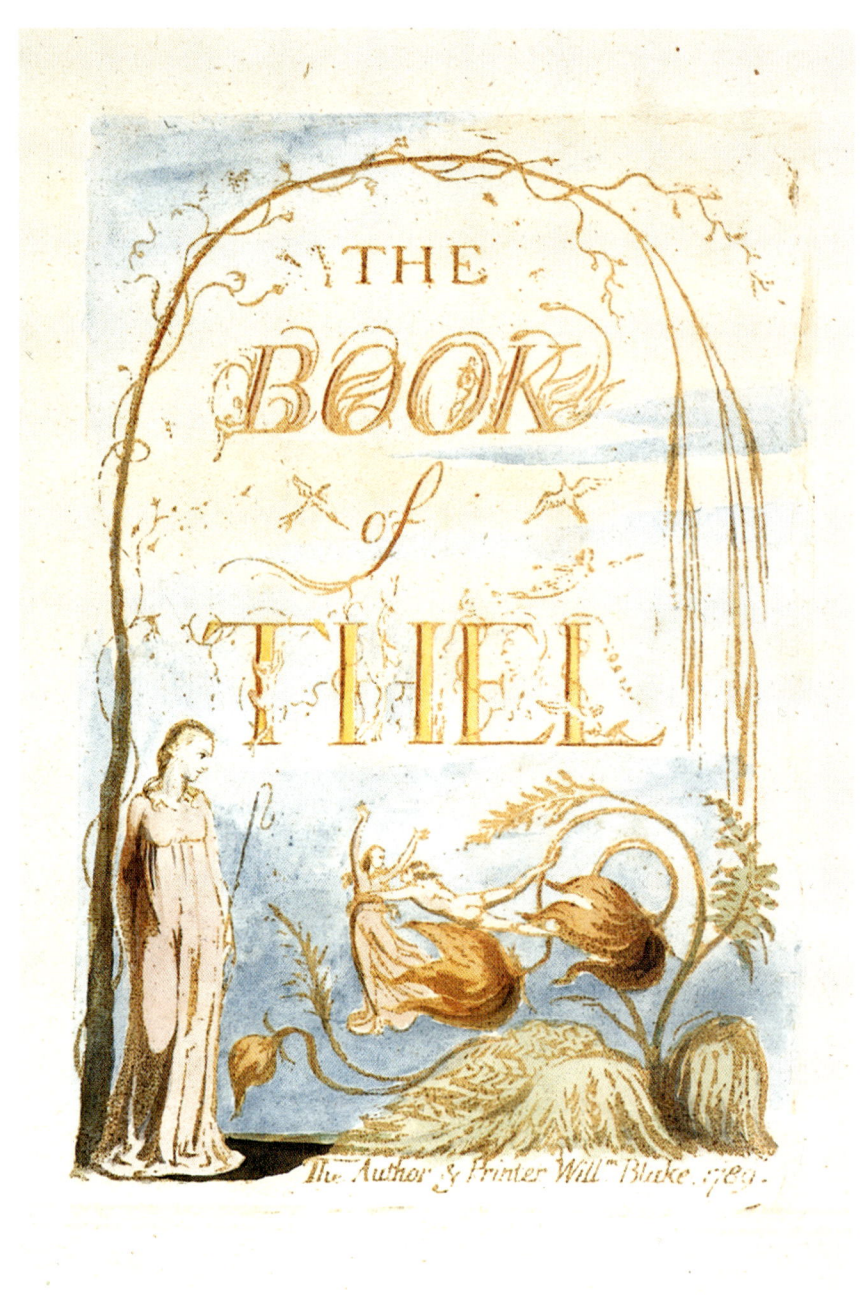

The Book of Thel, Copy B, title page,
relief etching with pen and ink and watercolor

But he that loves the lowly, pours his oil upon my head,
And kisses me, and binds his nuptial bands around my breast,
And says: Thou mother of my children, I have loved thee,
And I have given thee a crown that none can take away.
But how this is sweet maid, I know not, and I cannot know,
I ponder, and I cannot ponder; yet I live and love.

The daughter of beauty wip'd her pitying tears with her white veil,
And said, Alas! I knew not this, and therefore did I weep;
That God would love a Worm I knew, and punish the evil foot
That wilful, bruis'd its helpless form: but that he cherish'd it
With milk and oil, I never knew; and therefore did I weep,
And I complaind in the mild air, because I fade away,
And lay me down in thy cold bed, and leave my shining lot.

Queen of the vales, the matron Clay answerd; I heard thy sighs,
And all thy moans flew o'er my roof, but I have calld them down:
Wilt thou O Queen enter my house, 'tis given thee to enter,
And to return; fear nothing, enter with thy virgin feet.

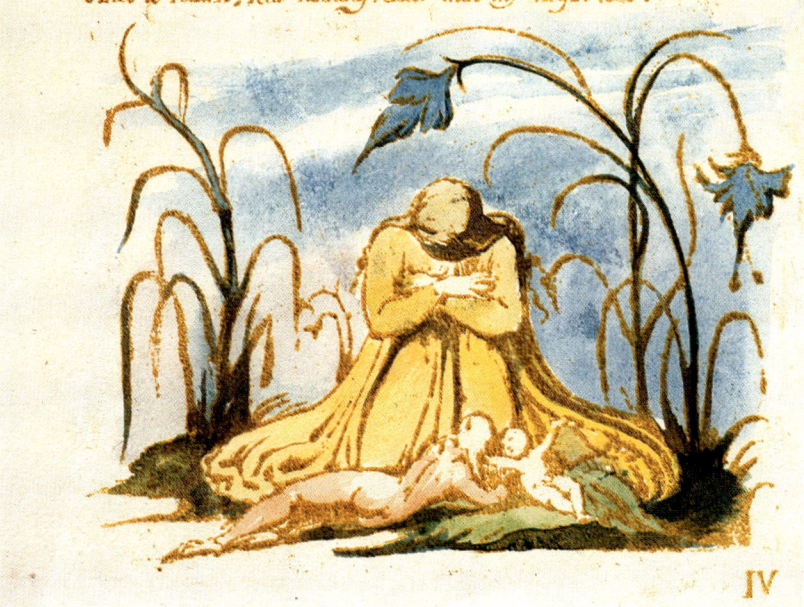

The Book of Thel, Copy R, pl. 7,
relief etching with pen and ink and watercolor

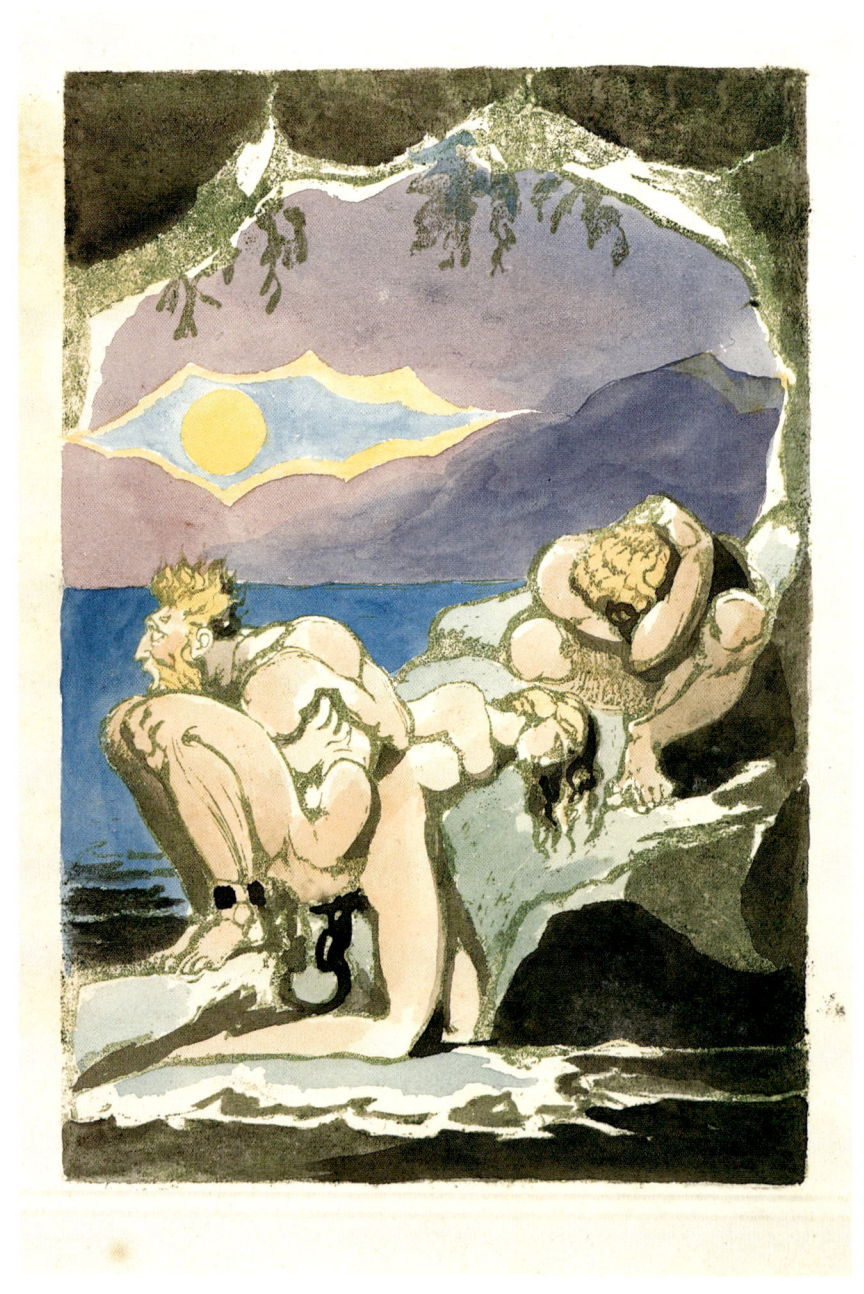

Visions of the Daughters of Albion, frontispiece,
relief etching with watercolor

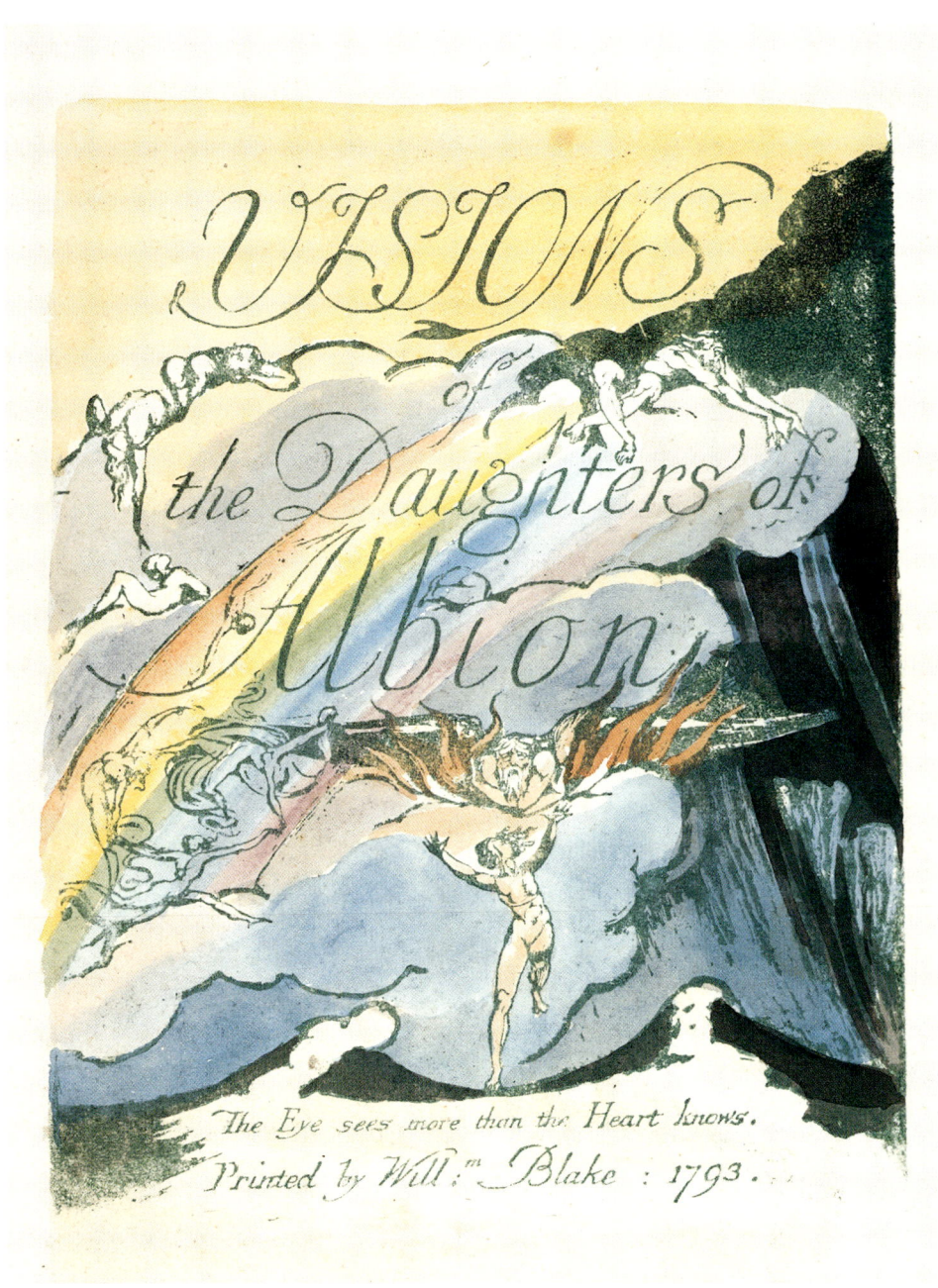

Visions of the Daughters of Albion, title page,
relief etching with watercolor

And none but Bromion can hear my lamentations.

With what sense is it that the chicken shuns the ravenous hawk?
With what sense does the tame pigeon measure out the expanse?
With what sense does the bee form cells? have not the mouse & frog
Eyes and ears and sense of touch? yet are their habitations.
And their pursuits, as different as their forms and as their joys:
Ask the wild ass why he refuses burdens: and the meek camel
Why he loves man: is it because of eye ear mouth or skin
Or breathing nostrils? No, for these the wolf and tyger have.
Ask the blind worm the secrets of the grave, and why her spires
Love to curl round the bones of death; and, ask the ravnous snake
Where she gets poison: & the wing'd eagle why he loves the sun
And then tell me the thoughts of man, that have been hid of old.

Silent I hover all the night, and all day could be silent.
If Theotormon once would turn his loved eyes upon me;
How can I be defild when I reflect thy image pure? (woe
Sweetest the fruit that the worm feeds on. & the soul prey'd on by
The new washd lamb ting'd with the village smoke & the bright swan
By the red earth of our immortal river: I bathe my wings.
And I am white and pure to hover round Theotormons breast.

Then Theotormon broke his silence. and he answered.

Tell me what is the night or day to one oerflowd with woe?
Tell me what is a thought? & of what substance is it made?
Tell me what is a joy? & in what gardens do joys grow?
And in what rivers swim the sorrows? and upon what mountains

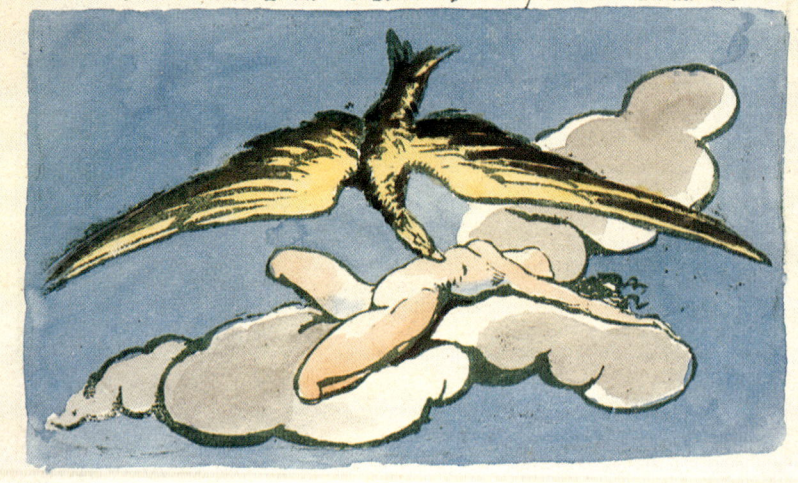

Visions of the Daughters of Albion, pl. 6,
relief etching with watercolor

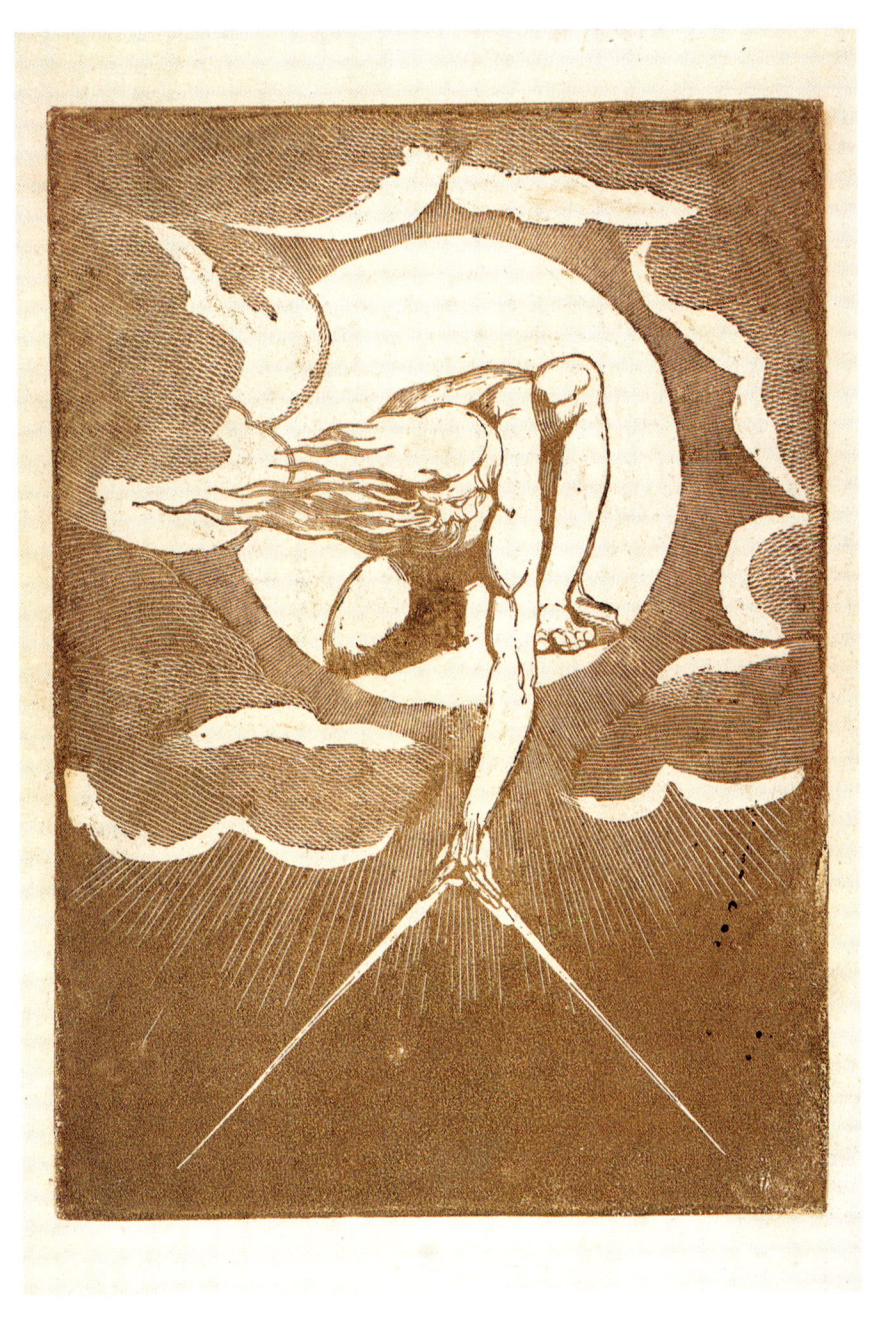

Europe. A Prophecy, frontispiece,
trial proof, relief etching

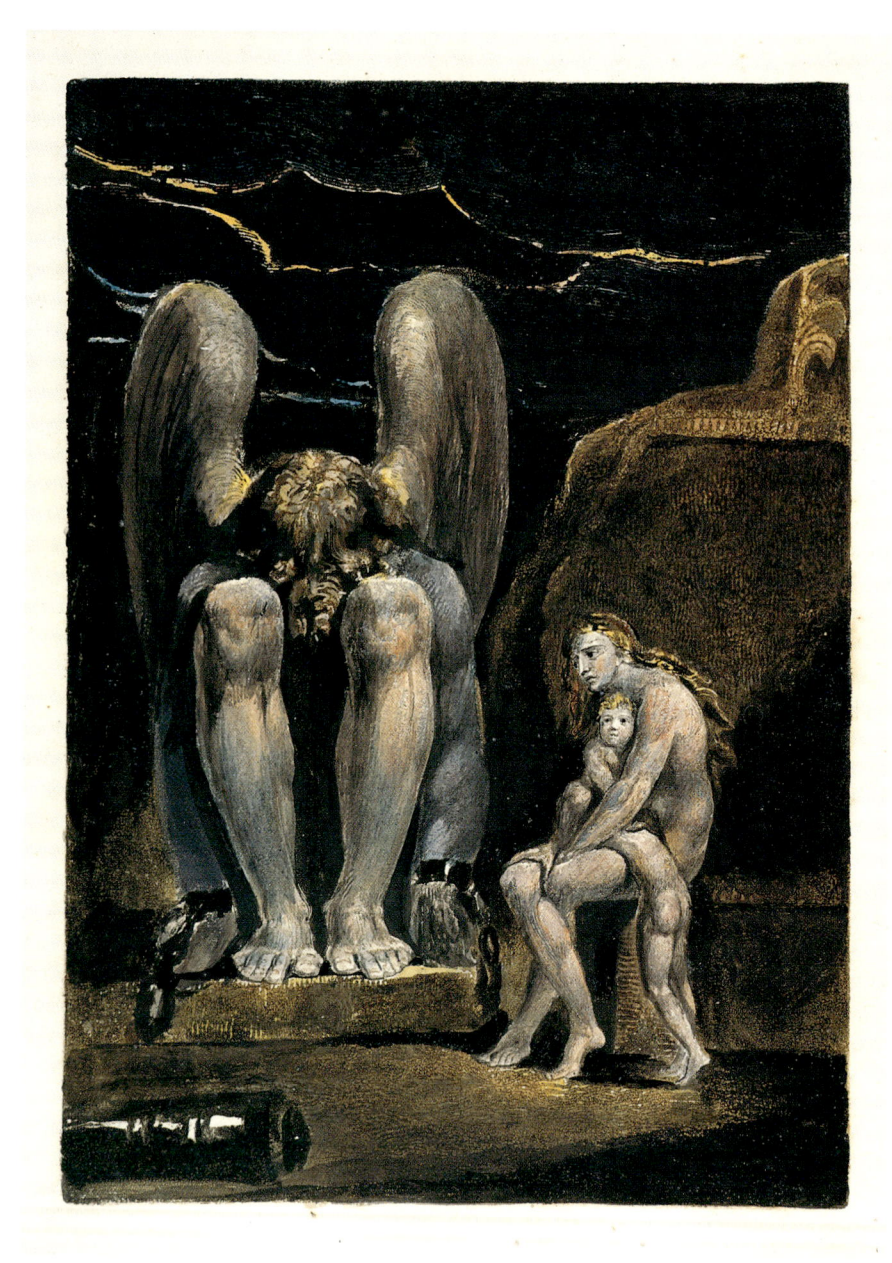

America. A Prophecy, frontispiece,
relief etching with pen and ink and watercolor

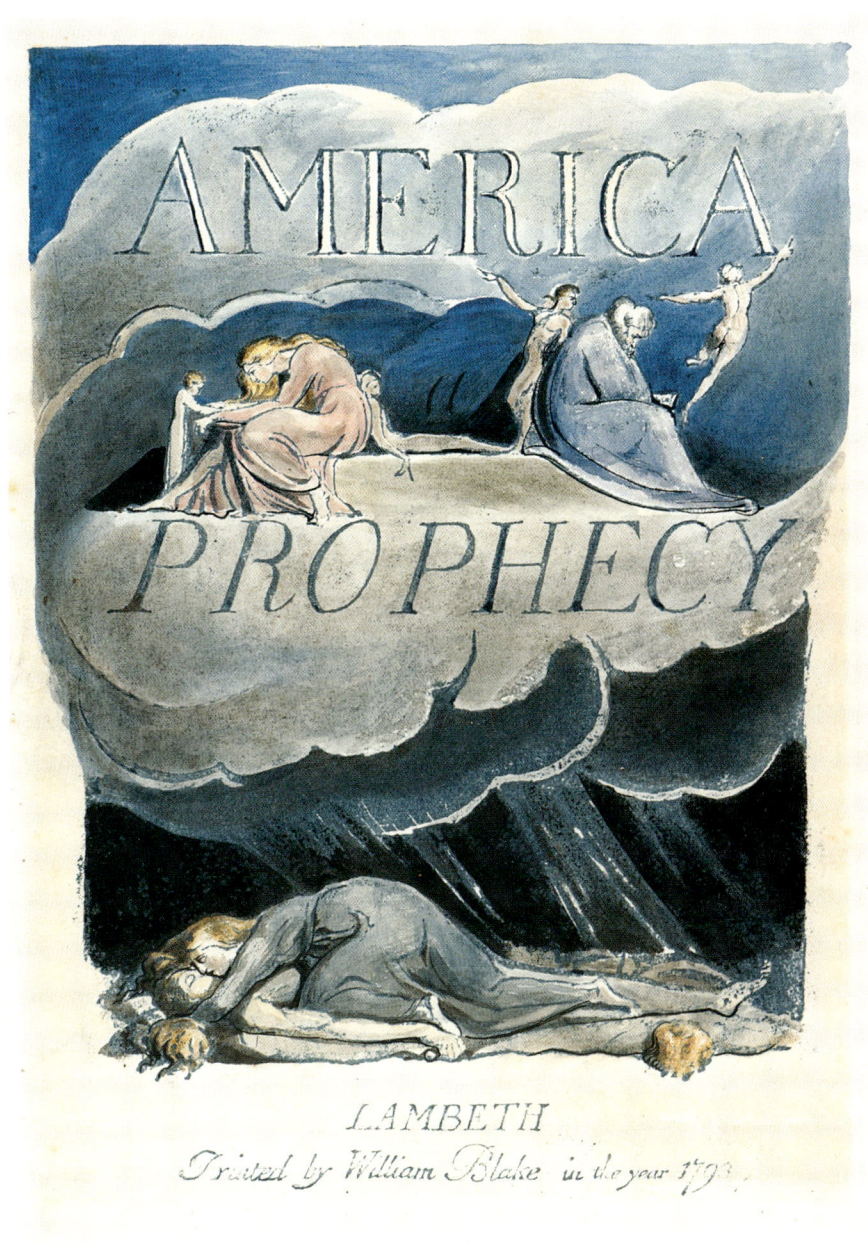

America. A Prophecy, title page,
relief etching with pen and ink and watercolor

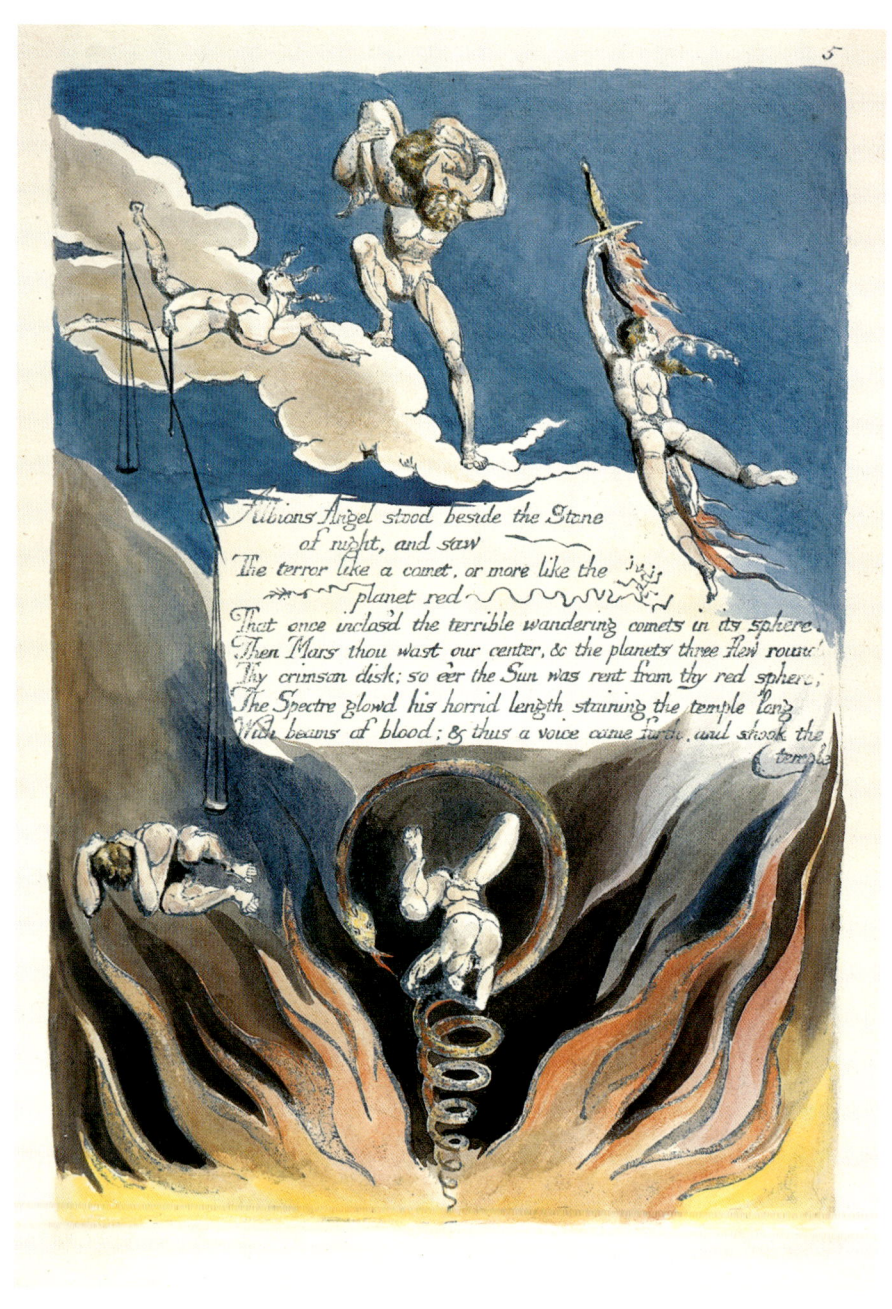

America. A Prophecy, pl. 7,
relief etching with pen and ink and watercolor

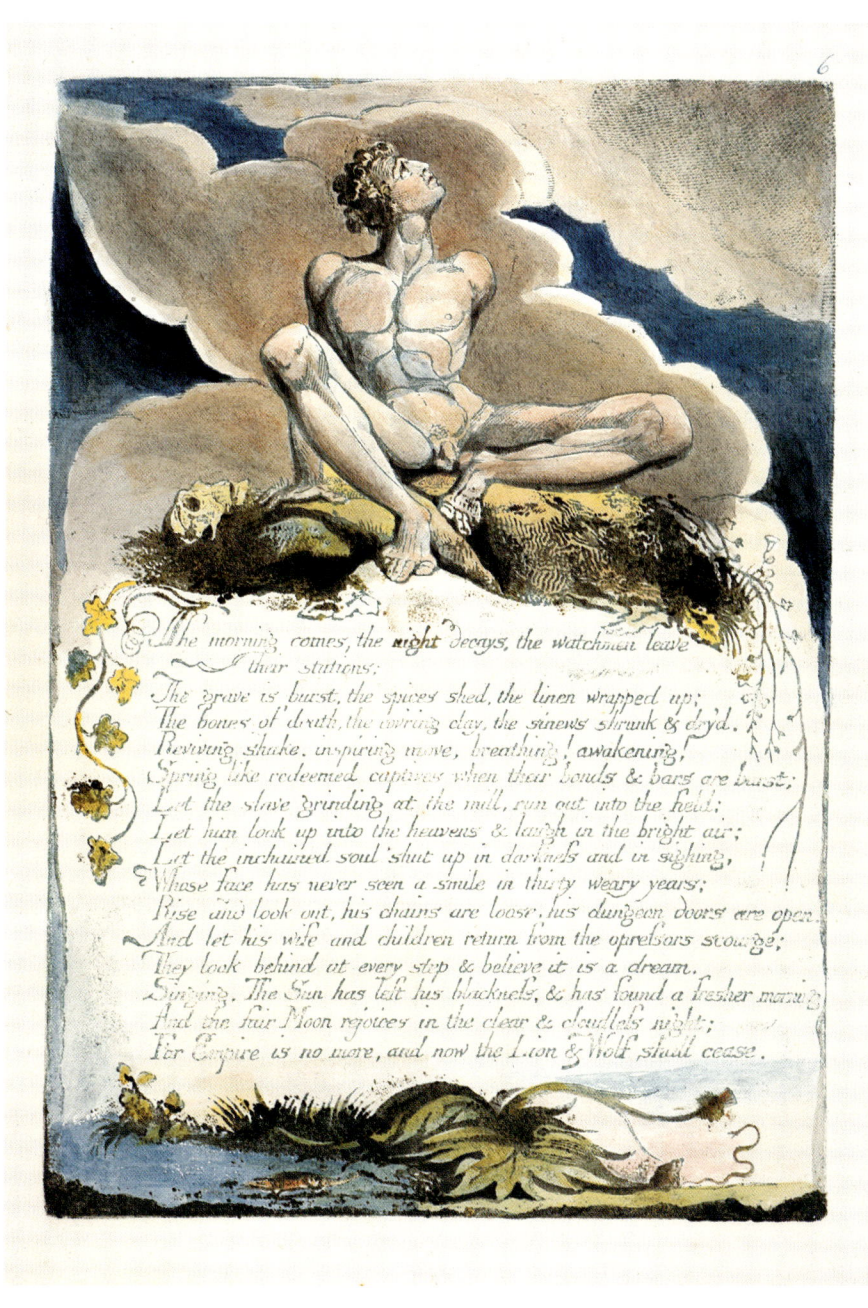

America. A Prophecy, pl. 8,
relief etching with pen and ink and watercolor

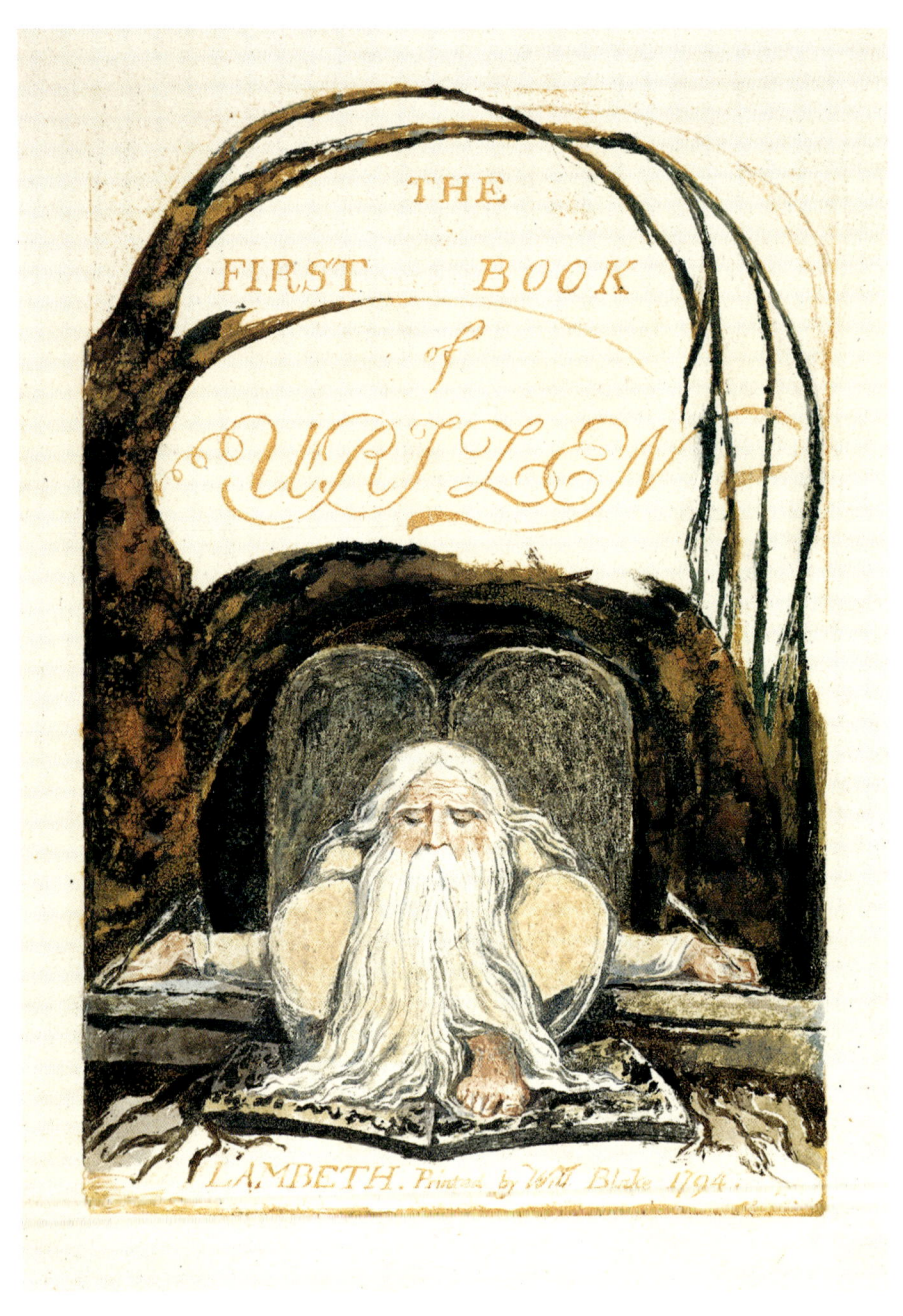

The [First] Book of Urizen, Copy C, title page,
color-printed relief etching with watercolor

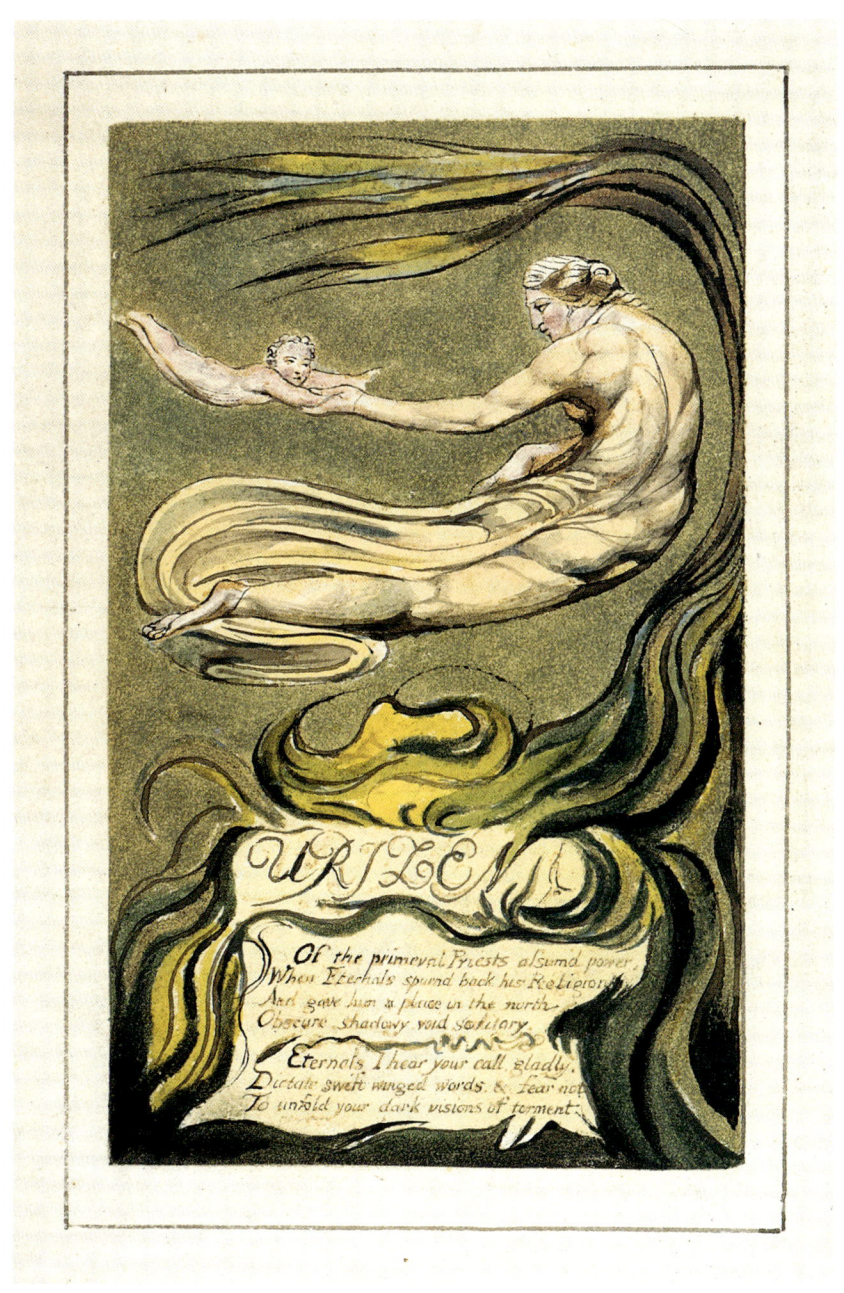

The [First] Book of Urizen, Copy C, Preludium,
relief etching with pen and ink and watercolor

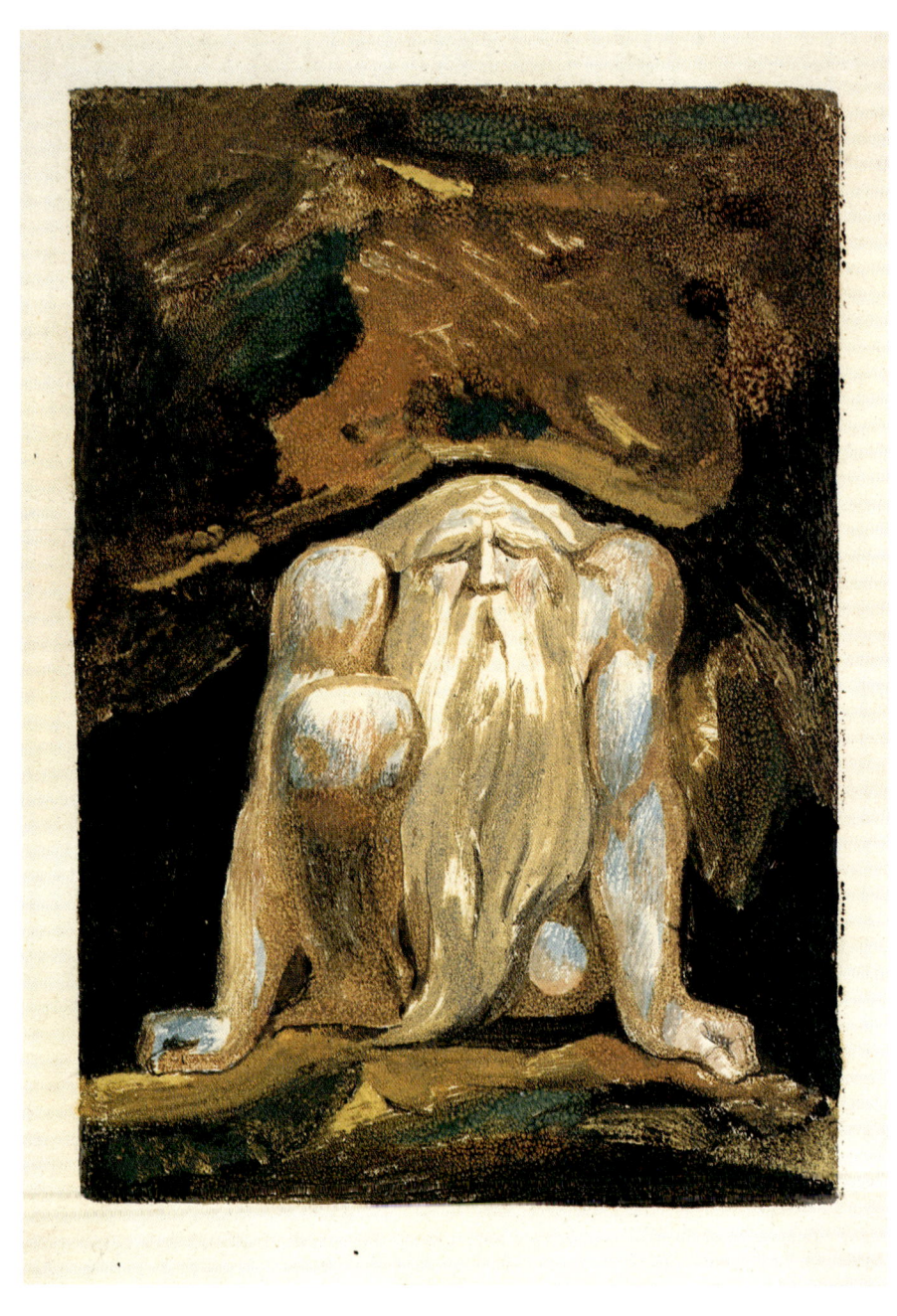

The [First] Book of Urizen, Copy C, pl. 8,
color-printed relief etching with watercolor

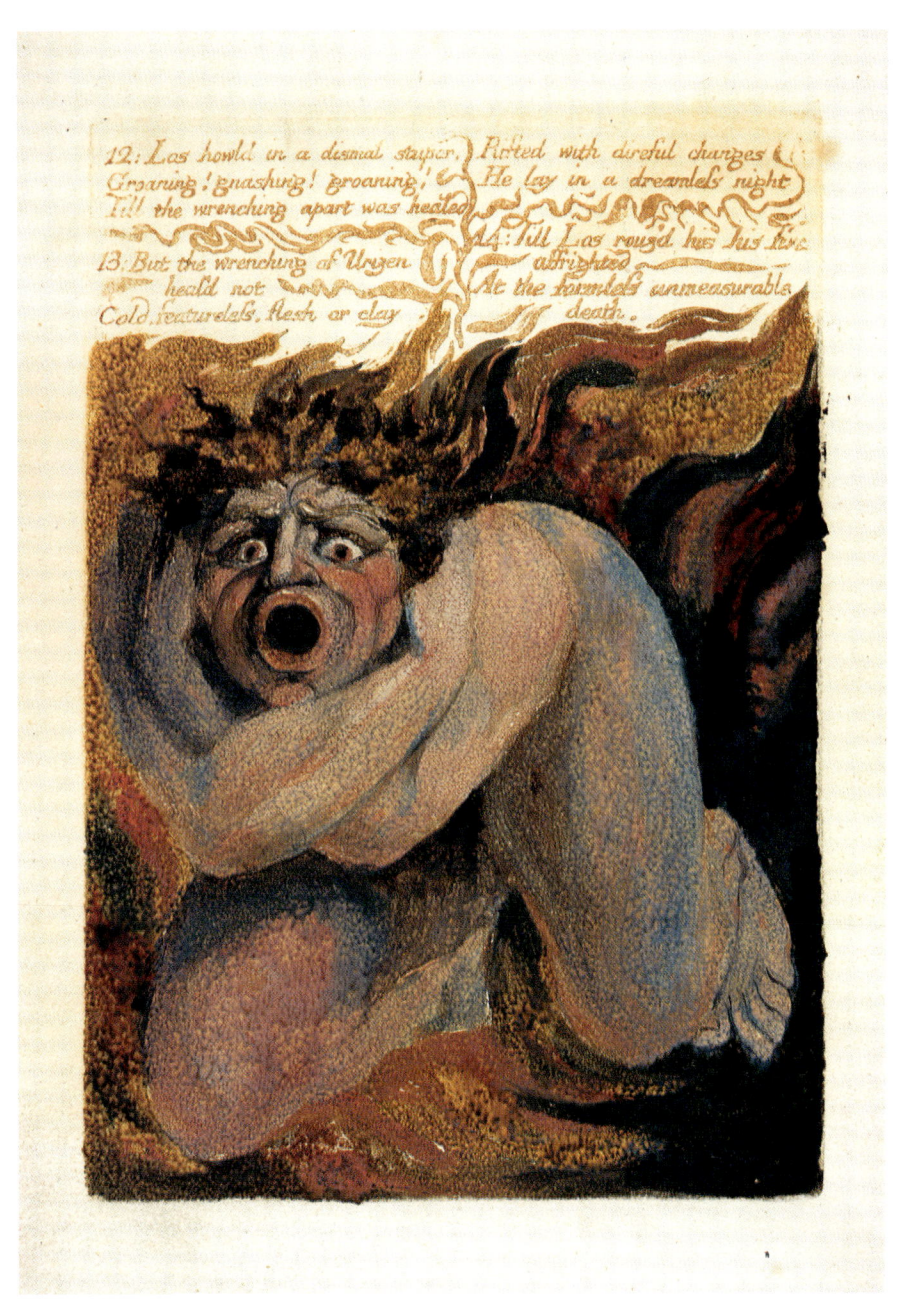

The [First] Book of Urizen, Copy A, pl. 10,
color-printed relief etching with watercolor

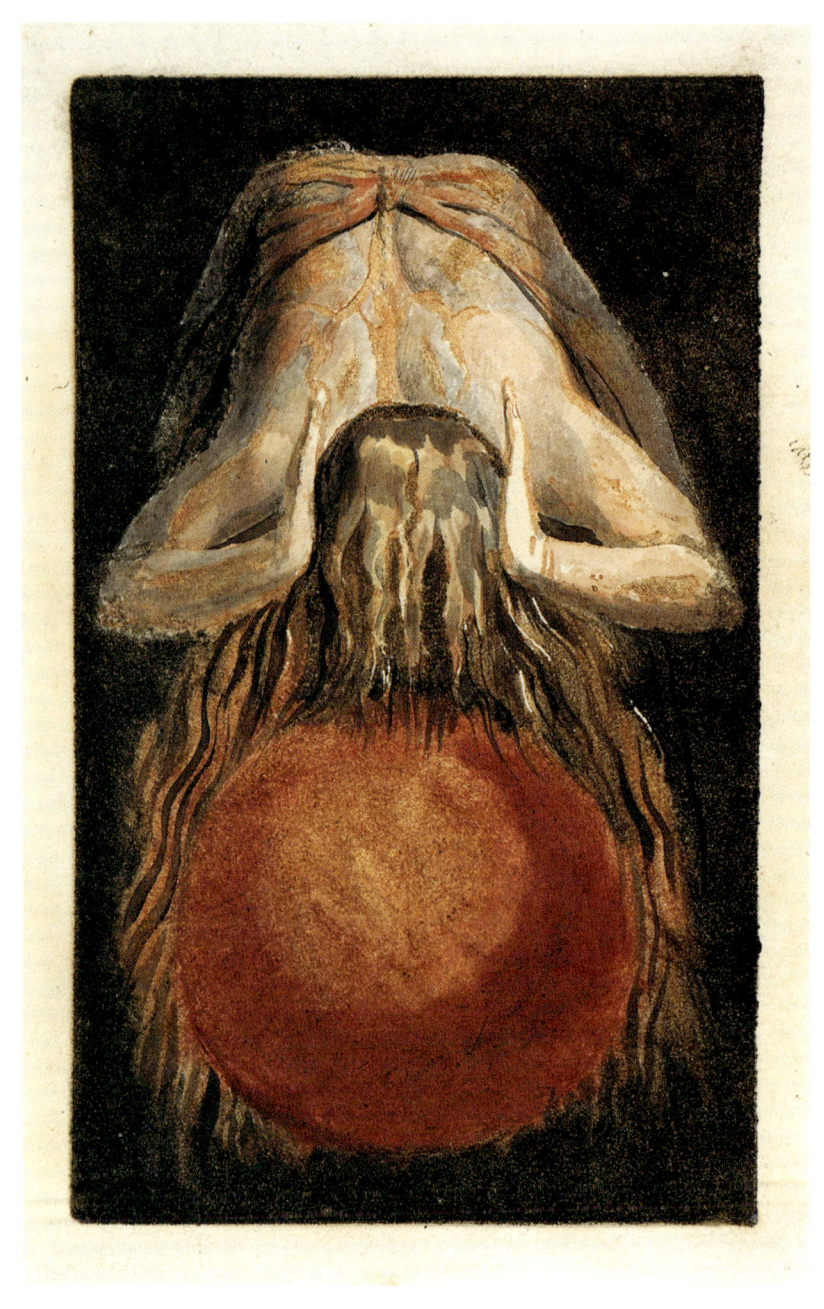

The [First] Book of Urizen, Copy A, pl. 11,
color-printed relief etching with watercolor

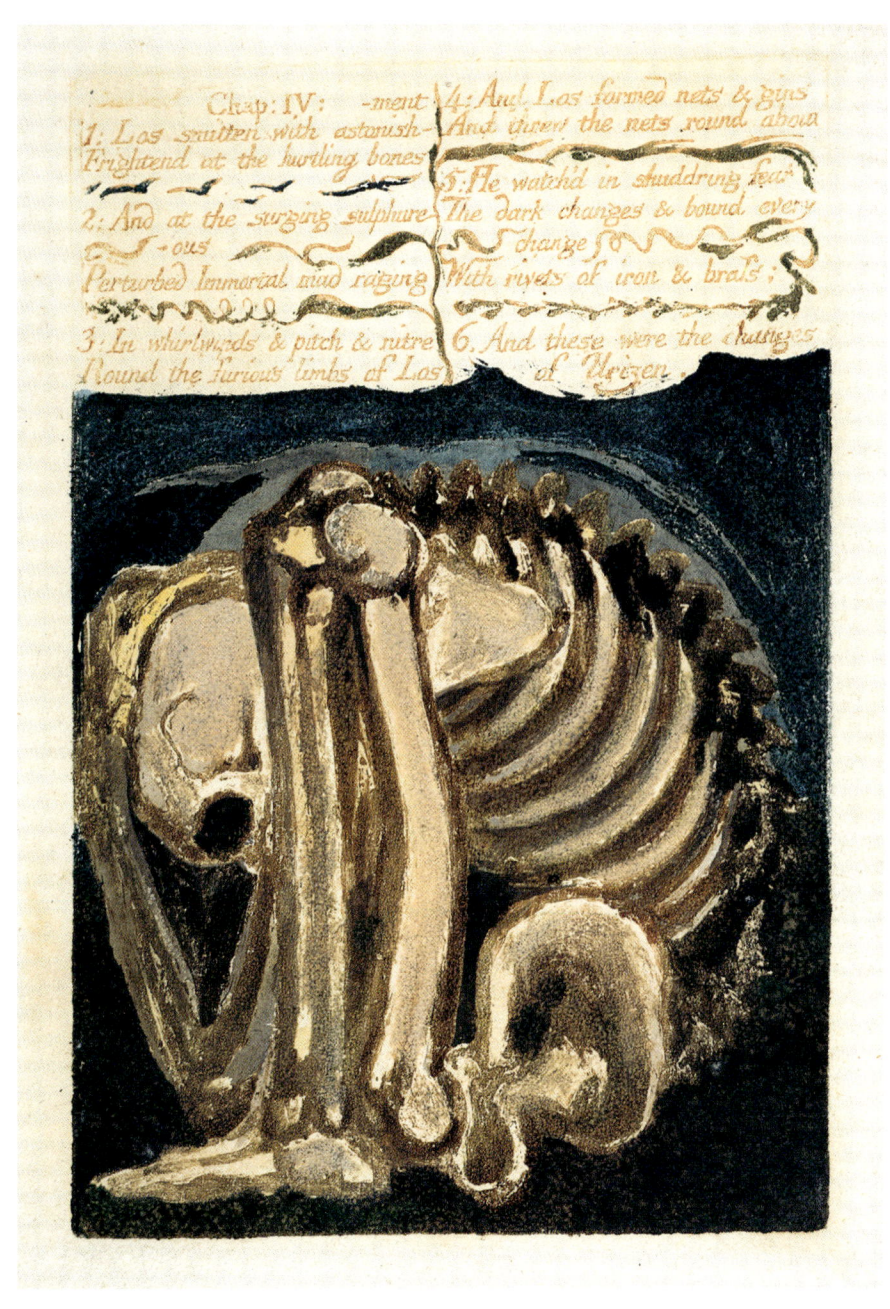

The [First] Book of Urizen, Copy A, pl. 12,
color-printed relief etching with watercolor

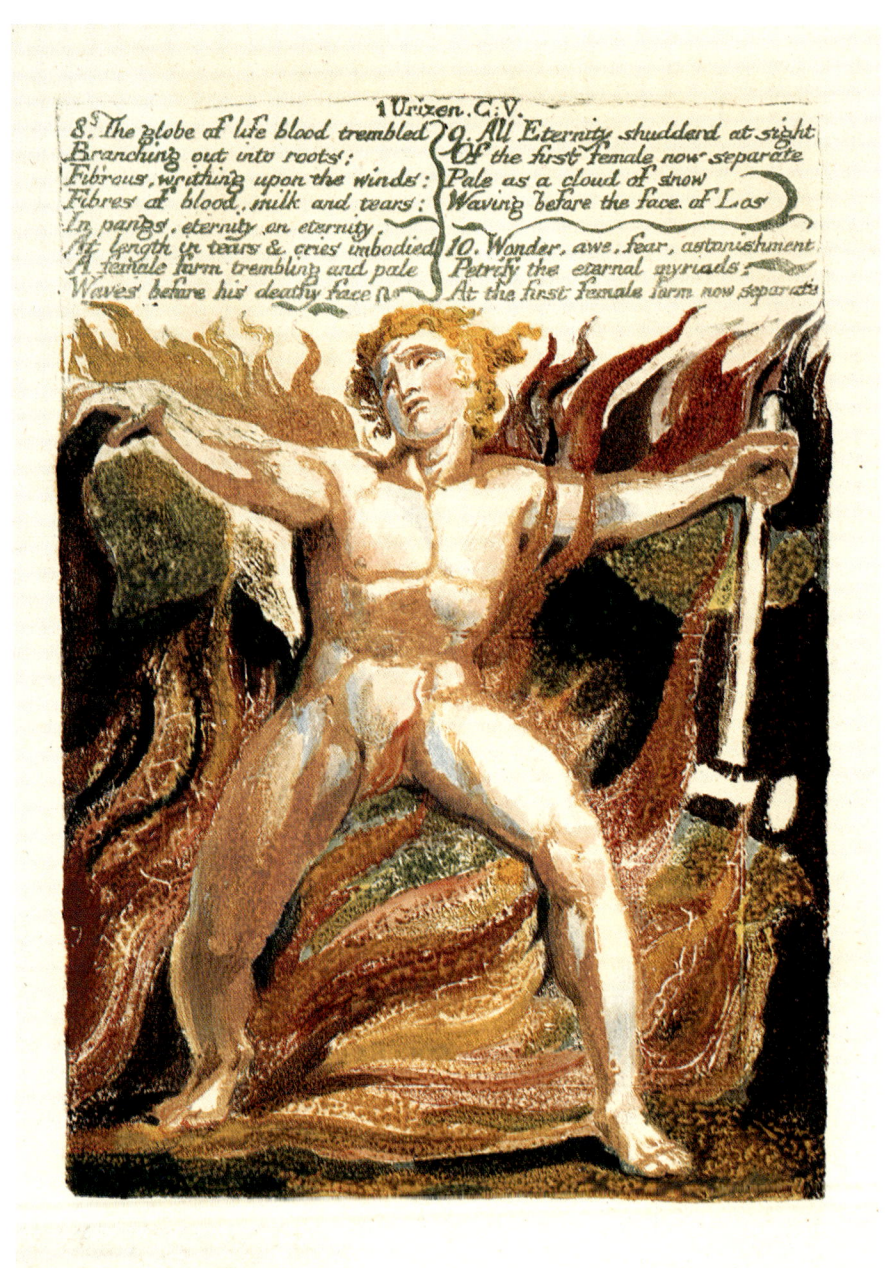

The [First] Book of Urizen, Copy C, pl. 15,
color-printed relief etching with watercolor

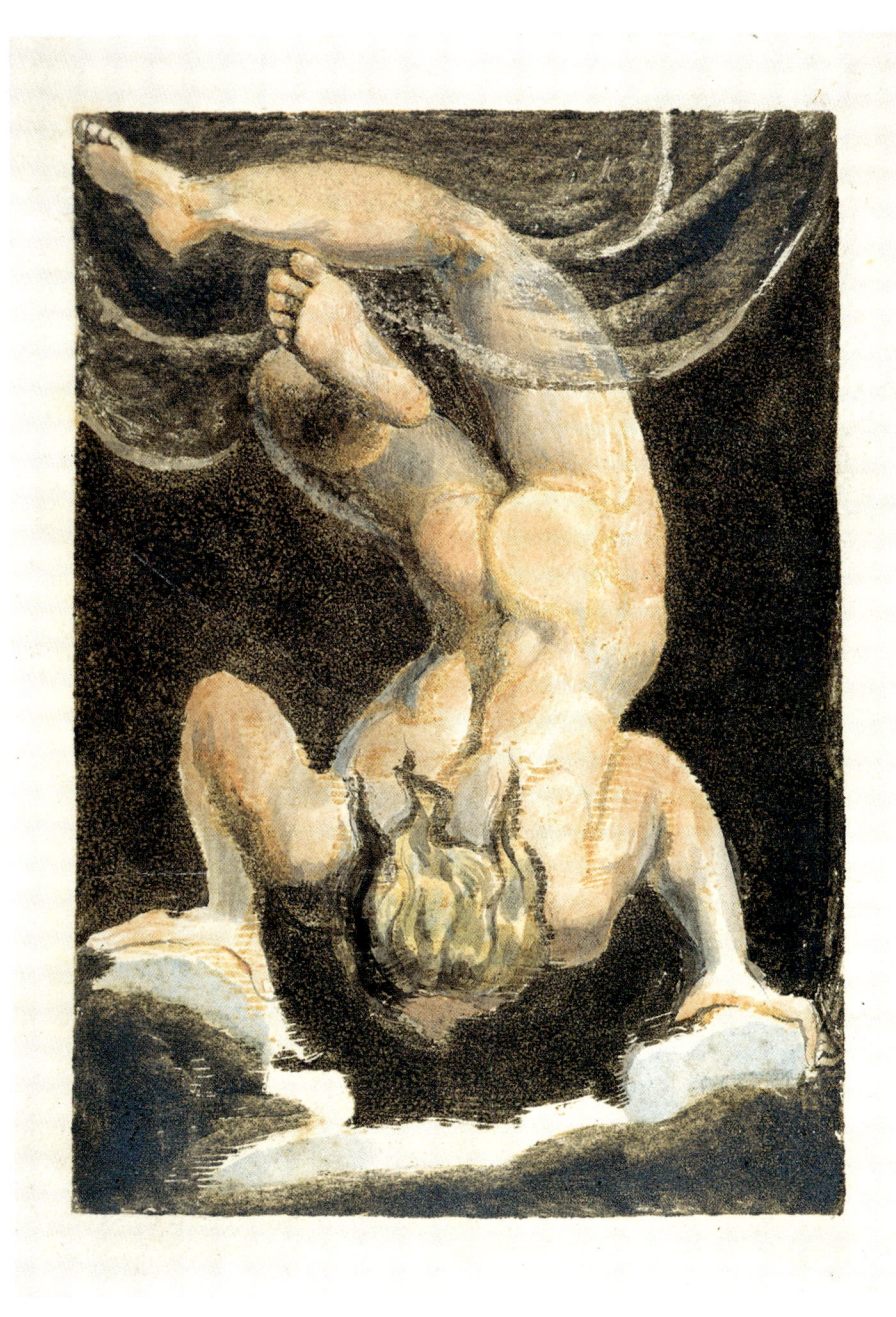

The [First] Book of Urizen, Copy A, pl. 15,
color-printed relief etching with watercolor

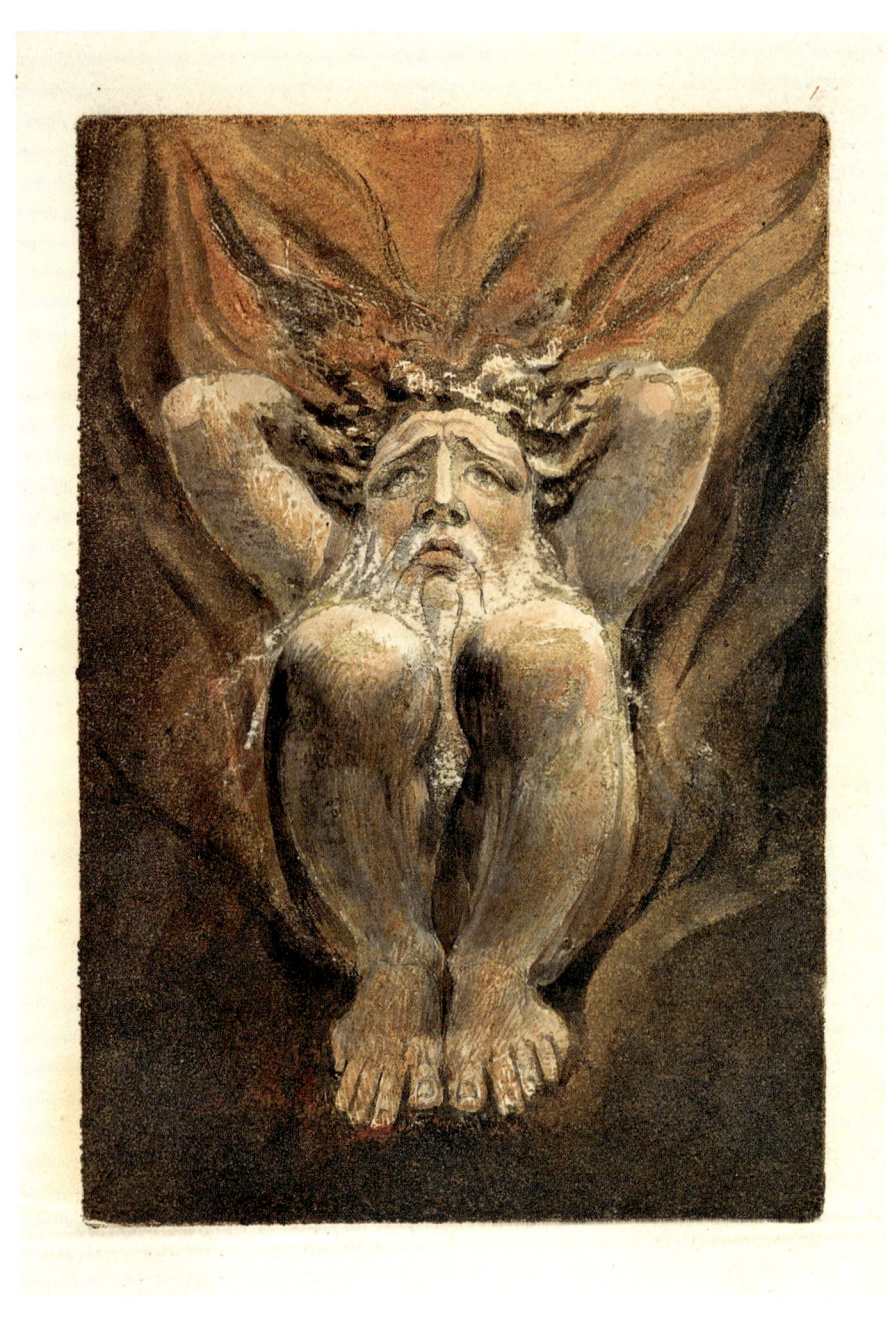

The [First] Book of Urizen, Copy A, pl. 21,
color-printed relief etching with watercolor

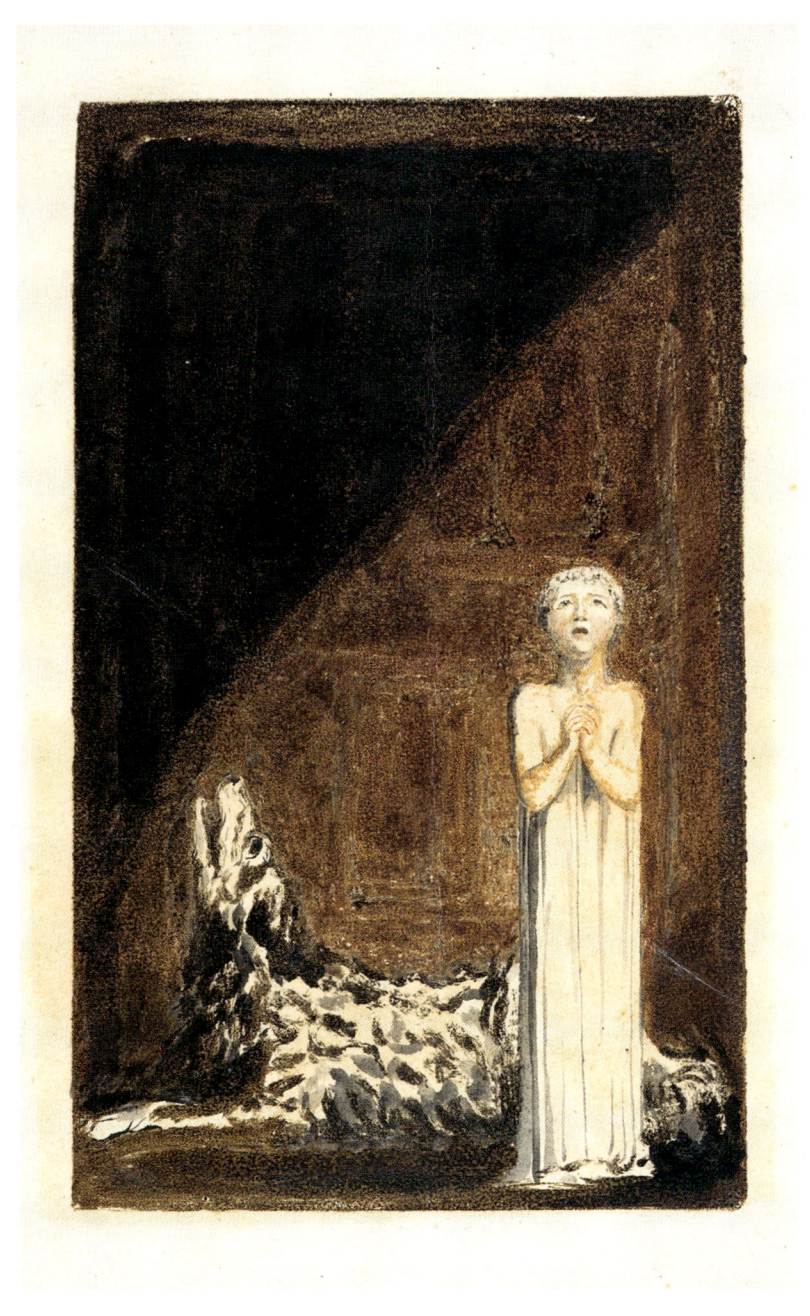

The [First] Book of Urizen, Copy A, pl. 25,
color-printed relief etching with watercolor

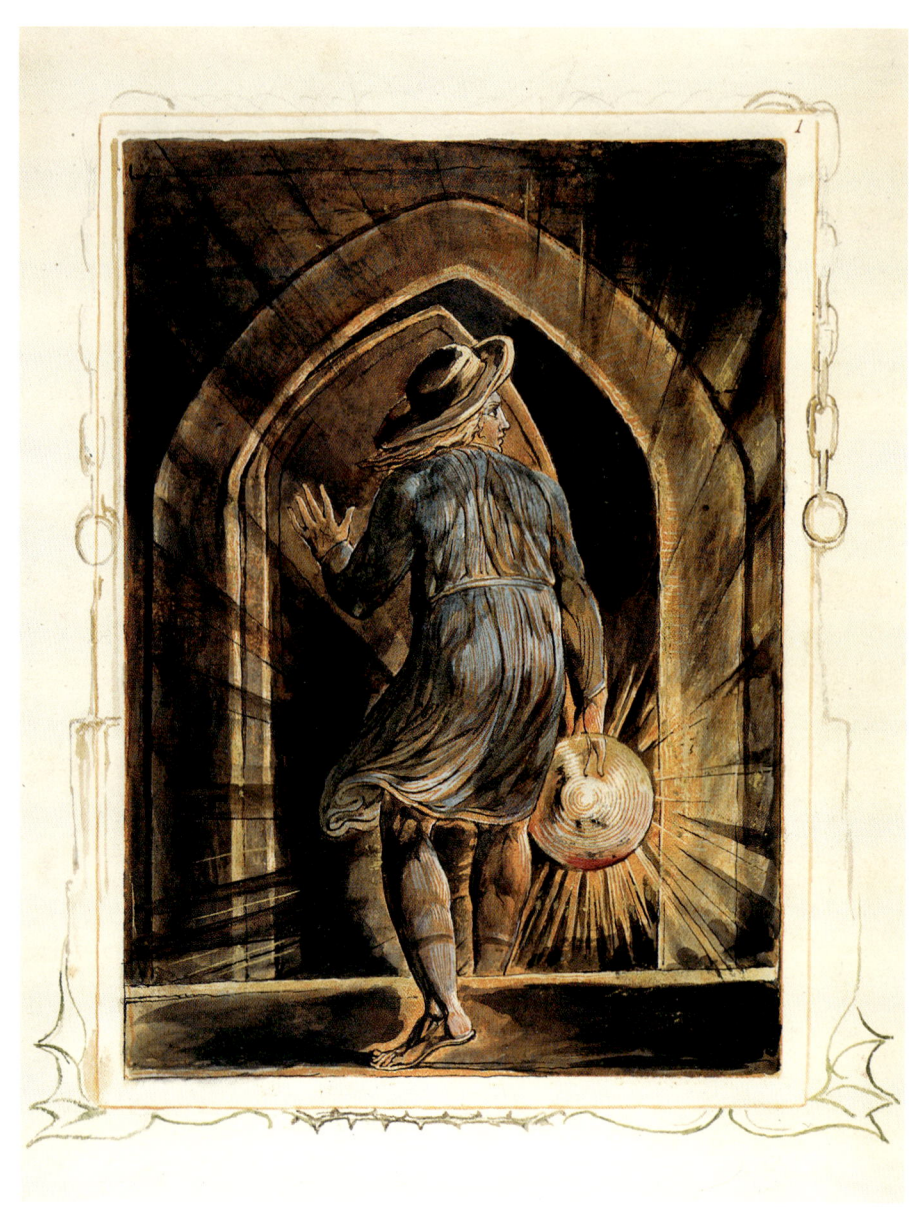

Jerusalem, frontispiece,
relief etching with pen and ink and watercolor

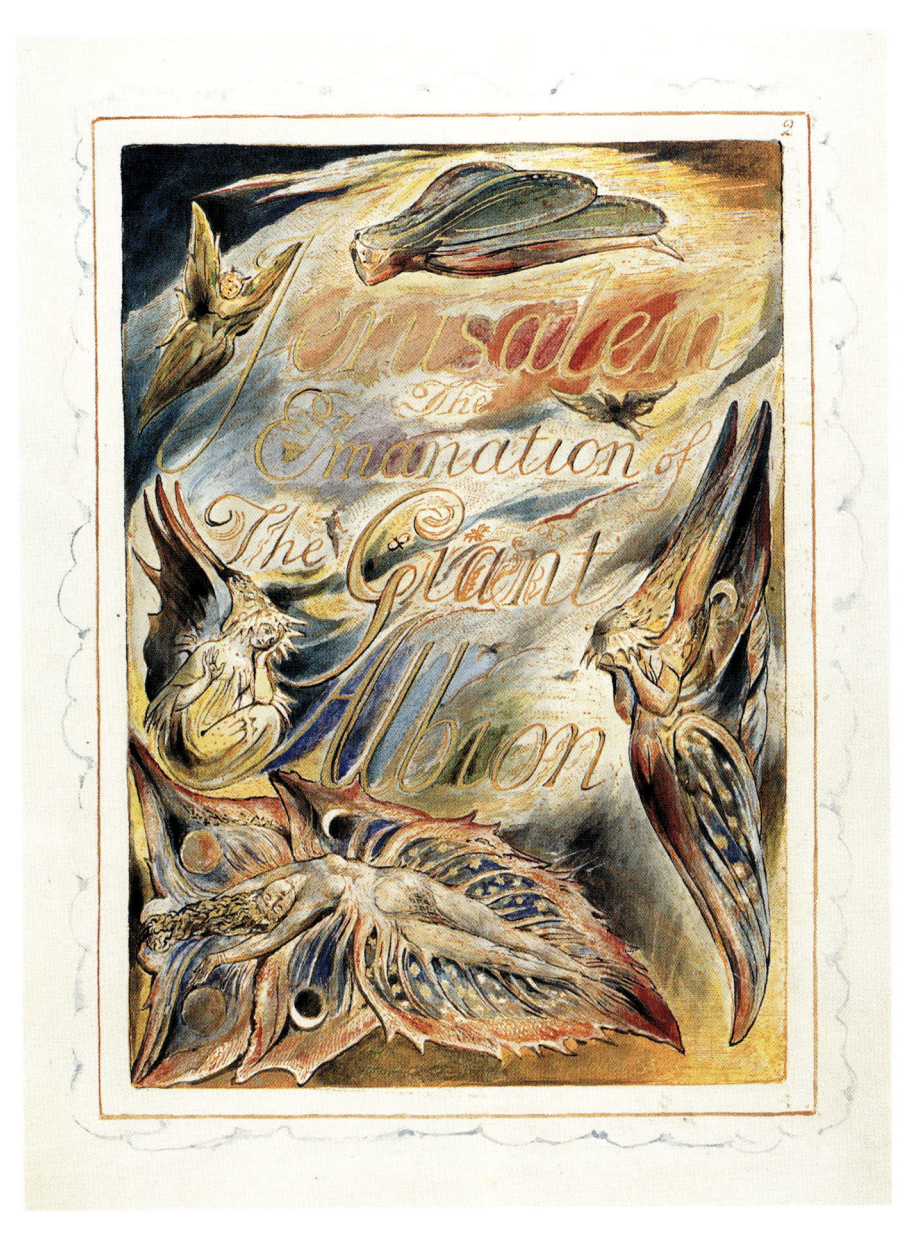

Jerusalem, title page,
relief etching with pen and ink and watercolor, touched with gold

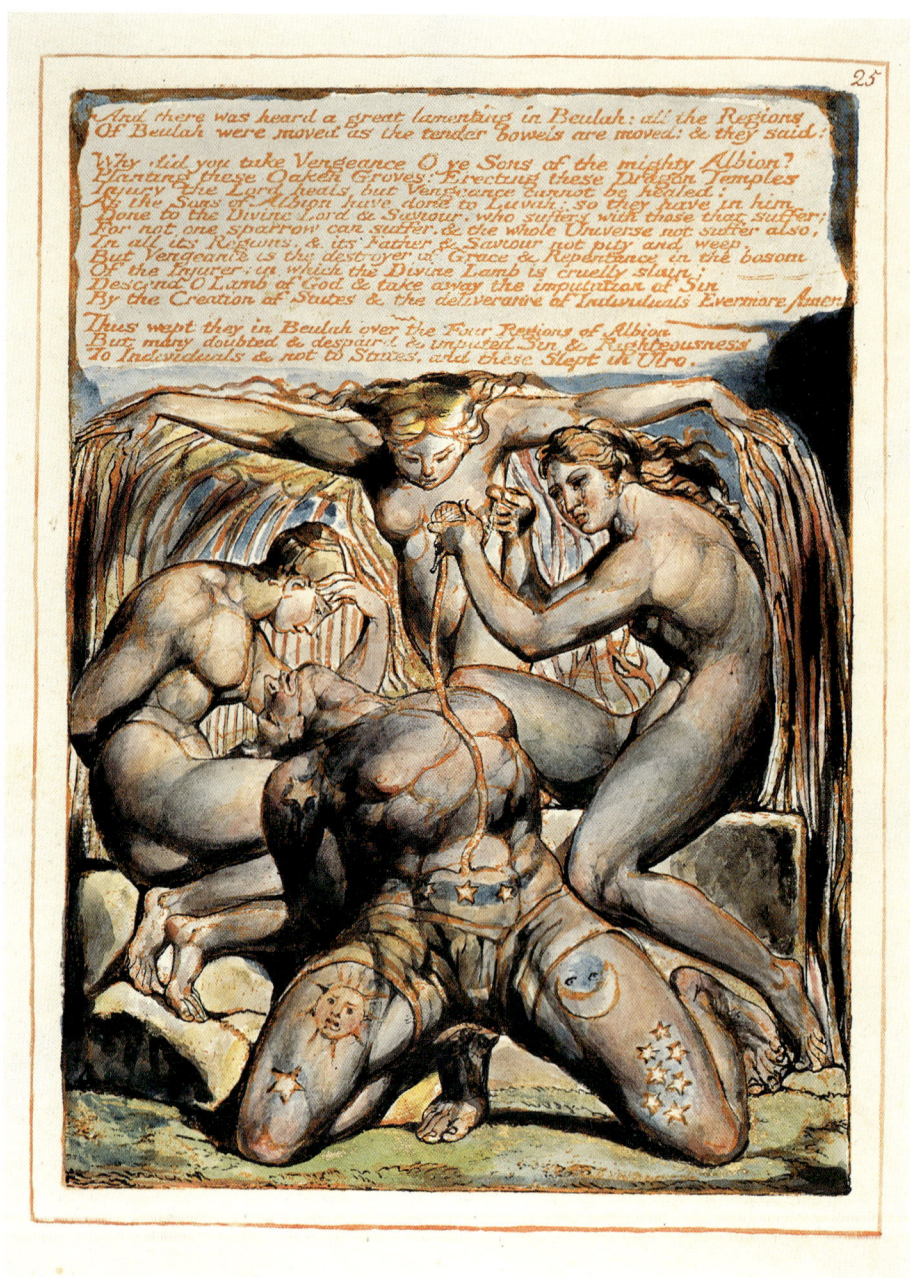

Jerusalem, pl. 25,
relief etching with pen and ink and watercolor, touched with gold

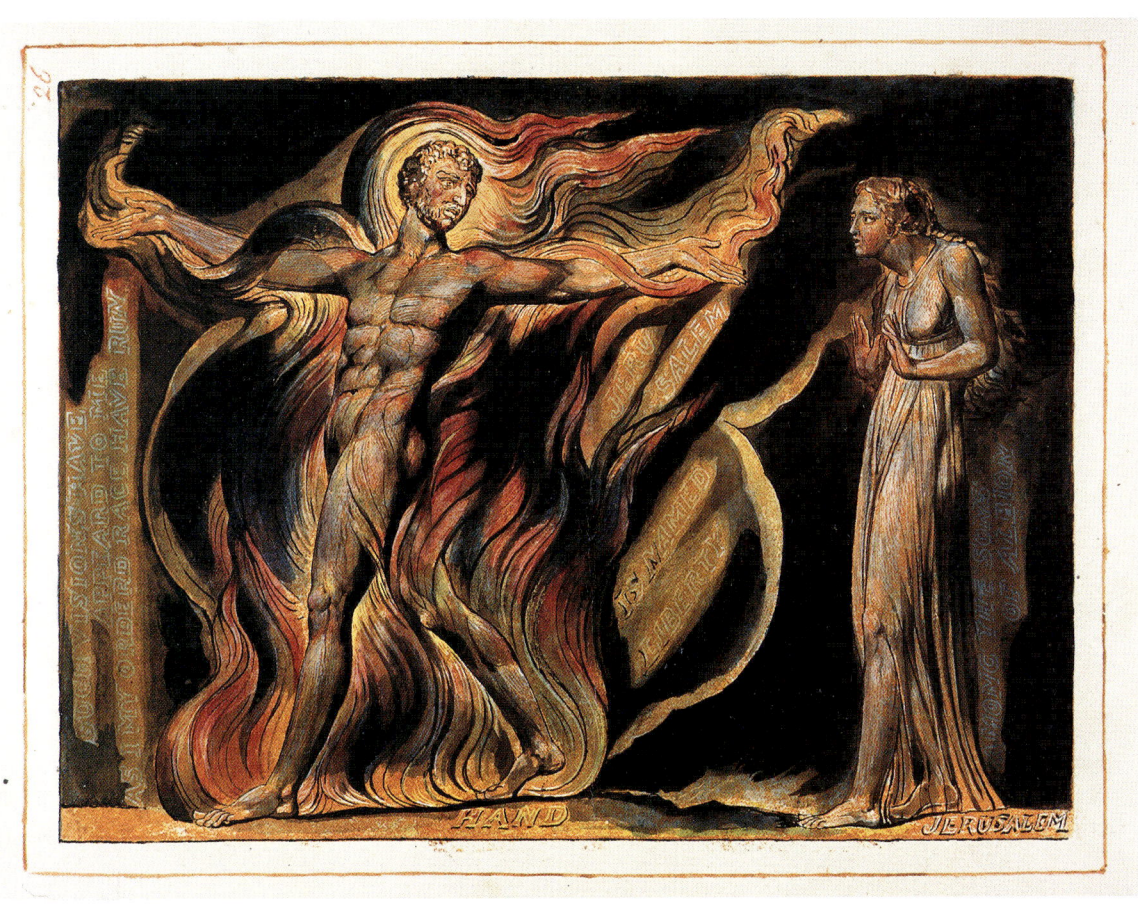

Jerusalem, pl. 26,
relief etching with pen and ink and watercolor

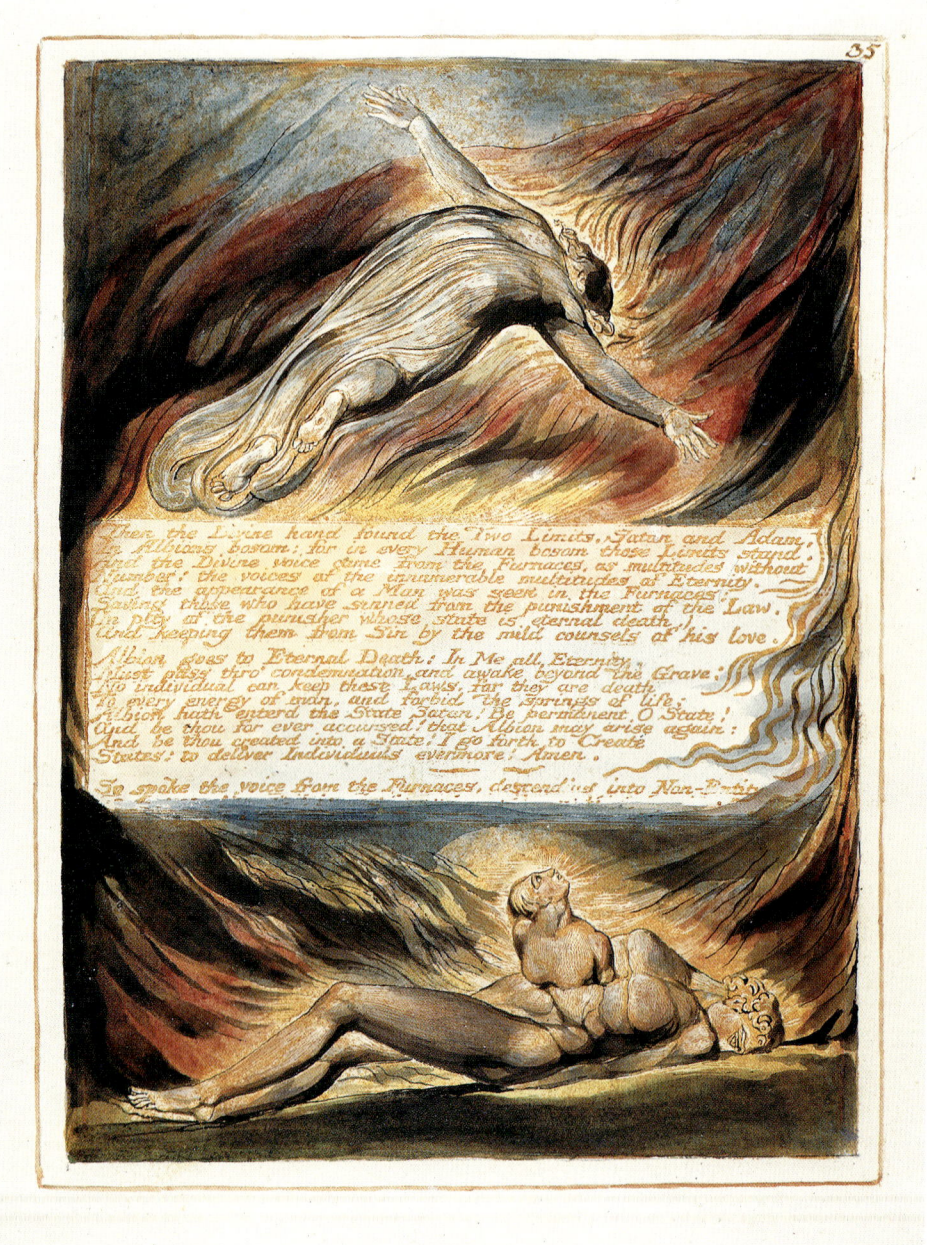

Jerusalem, pl. 35,
relief etching with pen and ink and watercolor

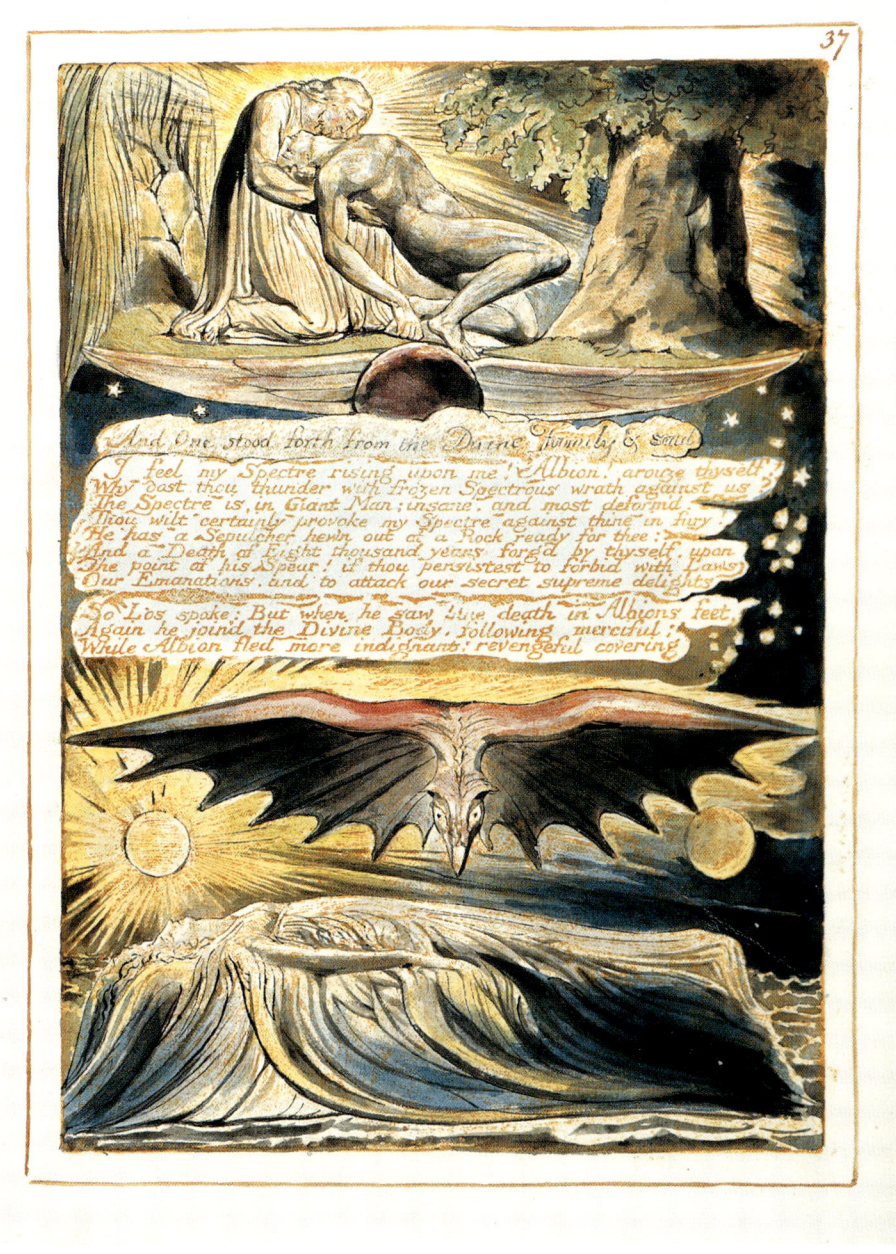

Jerusalem, pl. 37,
relief etching with pen and ink and watercolor

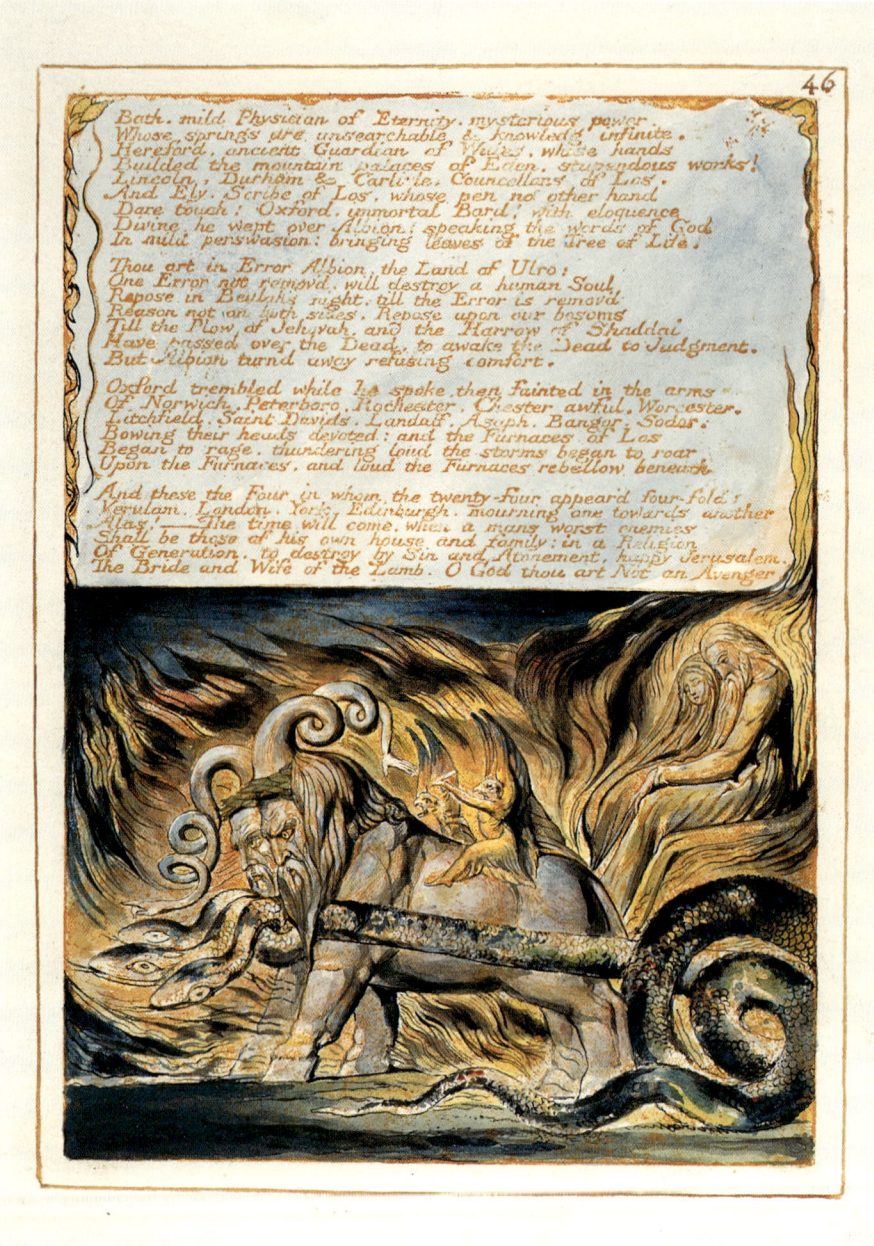

Jerusalem, pl. 46,
relief etching with pen and ink and watercolor

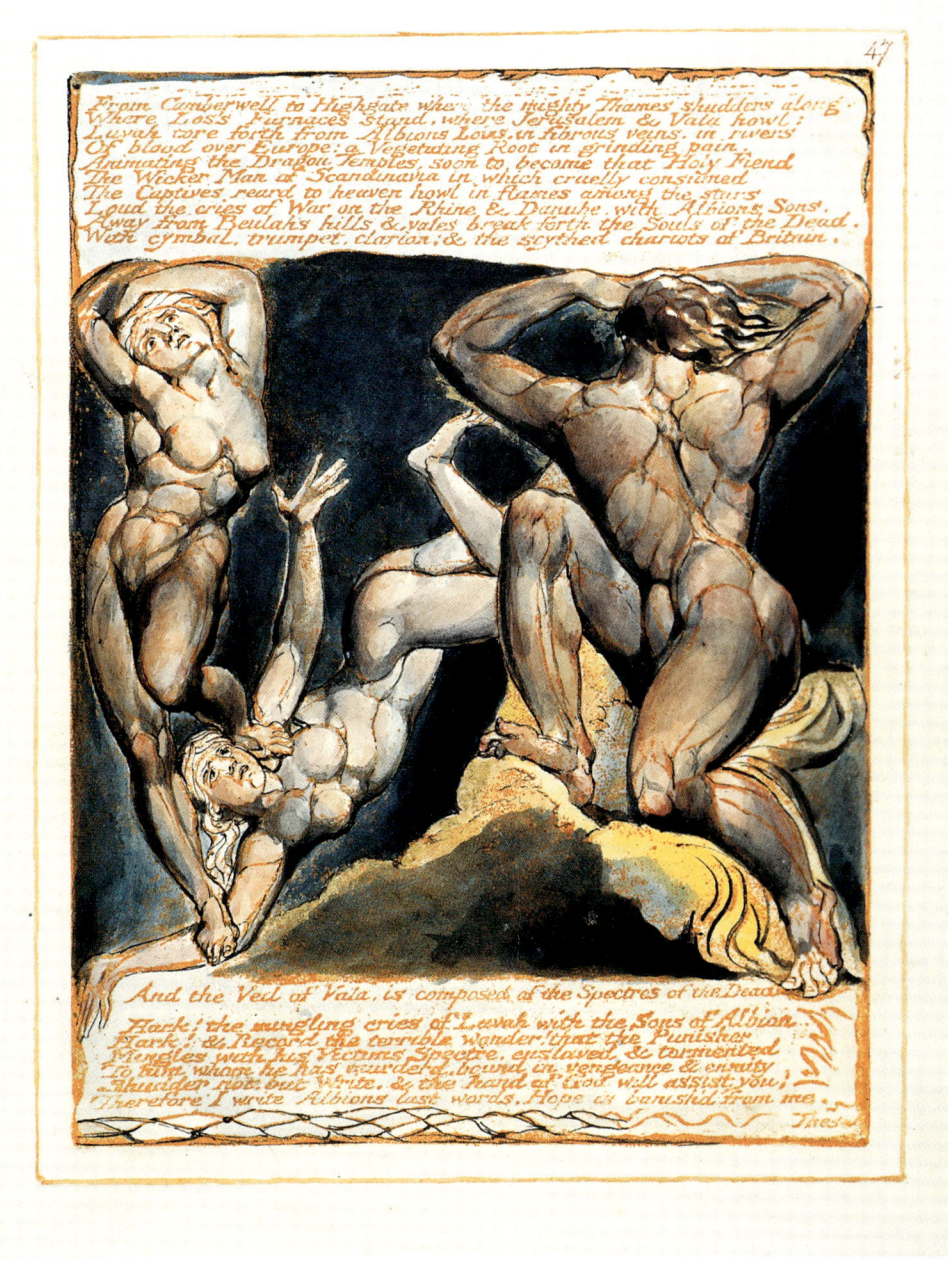

Jerusalem, pl. 47,
relief etching with pen and ink and watercolor

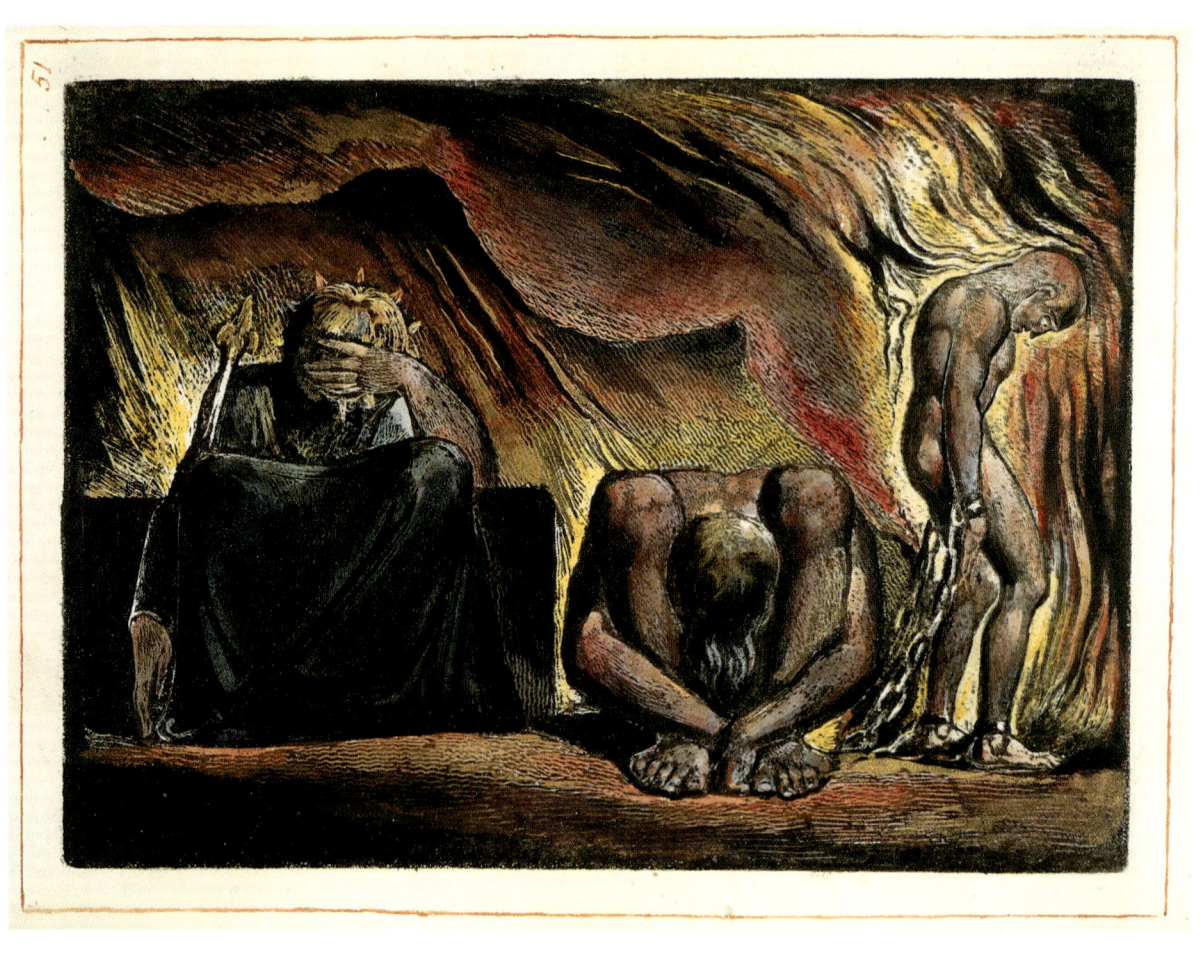

Jerusalem, pl. 51,
relief etching with pen and ink and watercolor

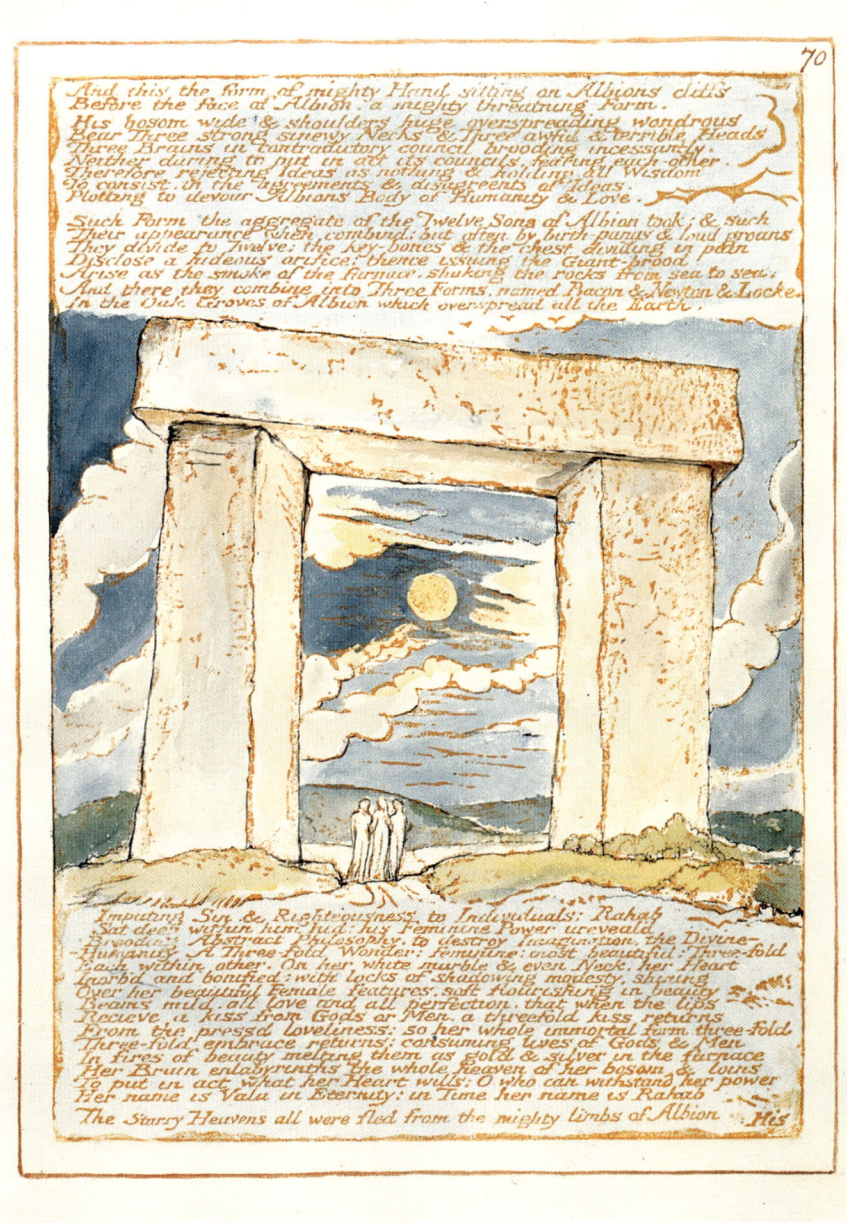

Jerusalem, pl. 70,
relief etching with pen and ink and watercolor

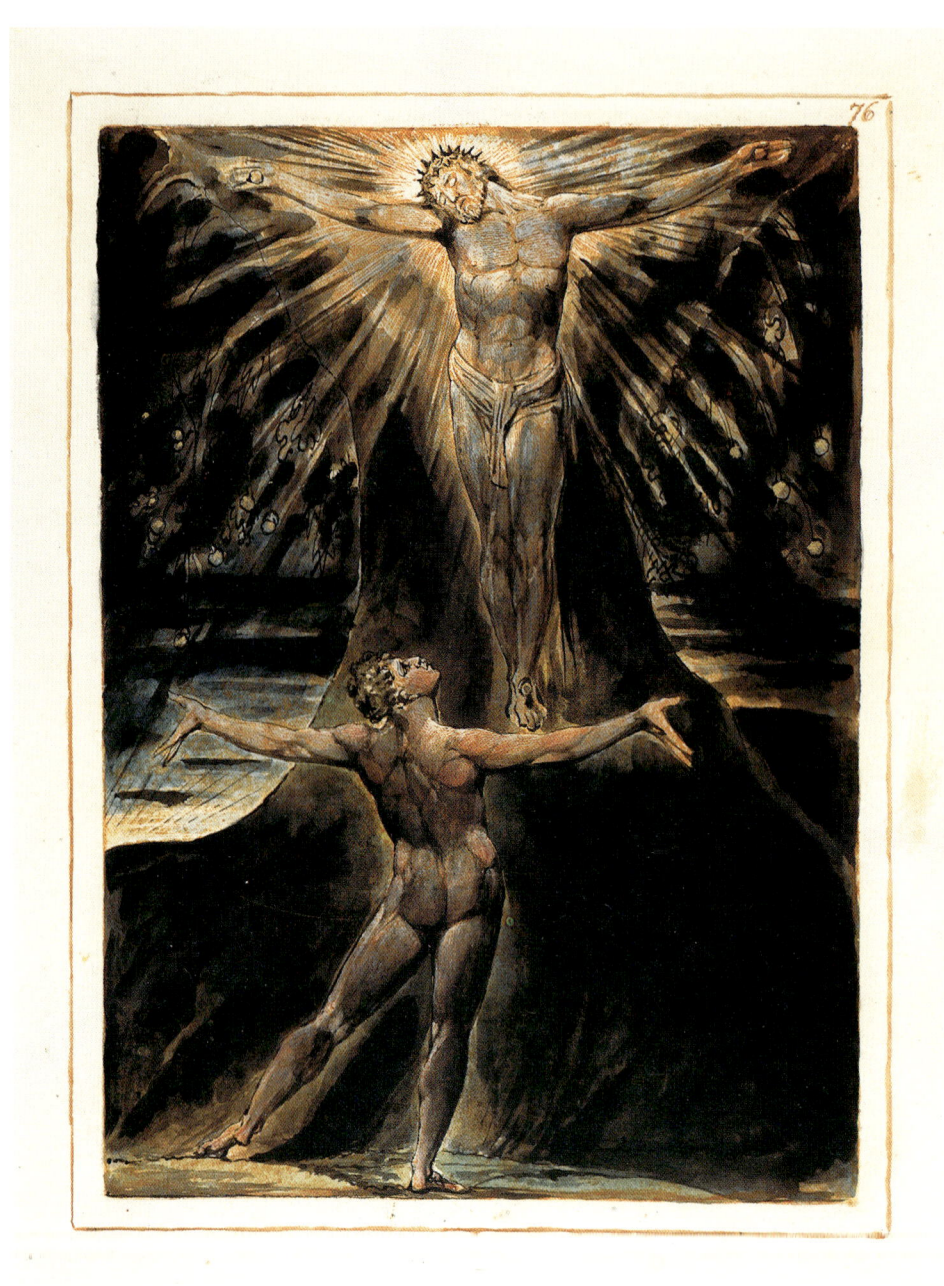

Jerusalem, pl. 76,
relief etching with pen and ink and watercolor

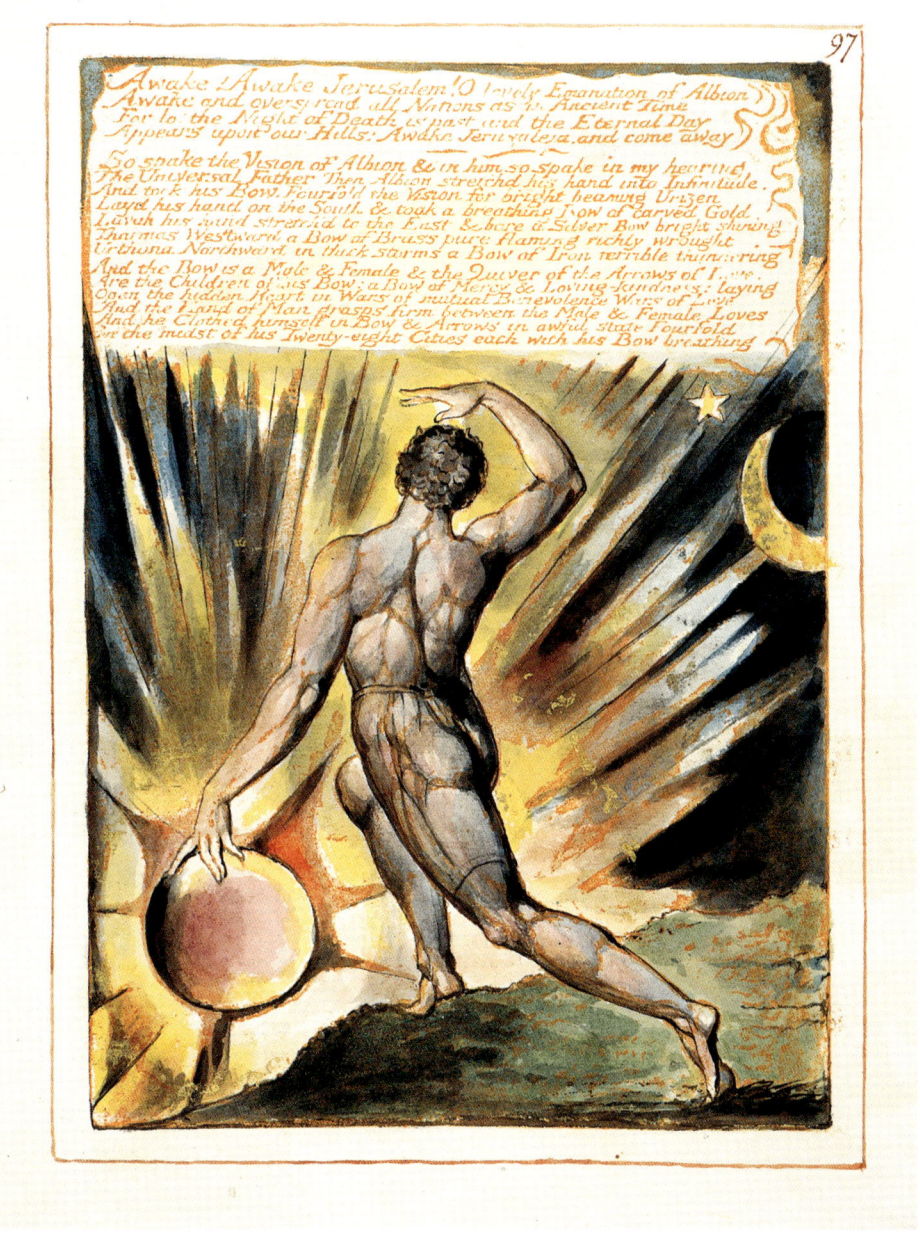

Jerusalem, pl. 97,
relief etching with pen and ink and watercolor

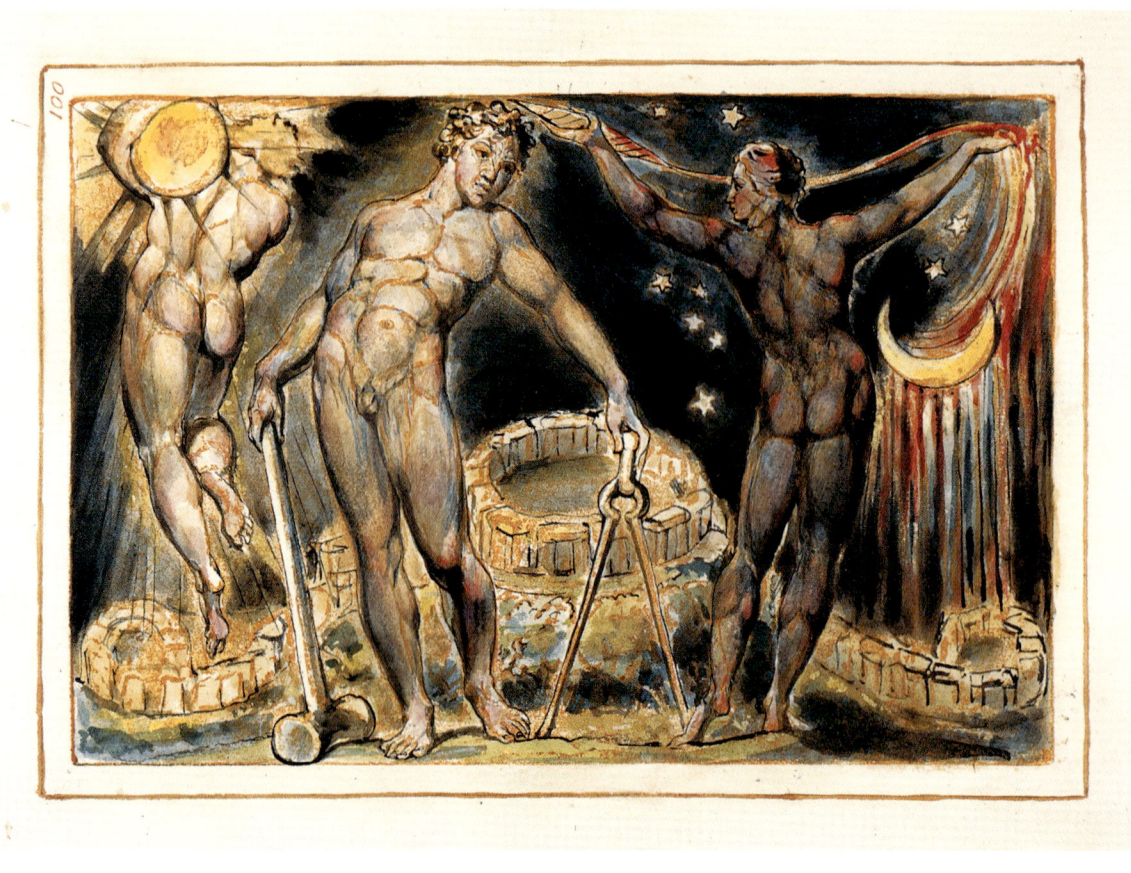

Jerusalem, pl. 100,
relief etching with pen and ink and watercolor, touched with gold

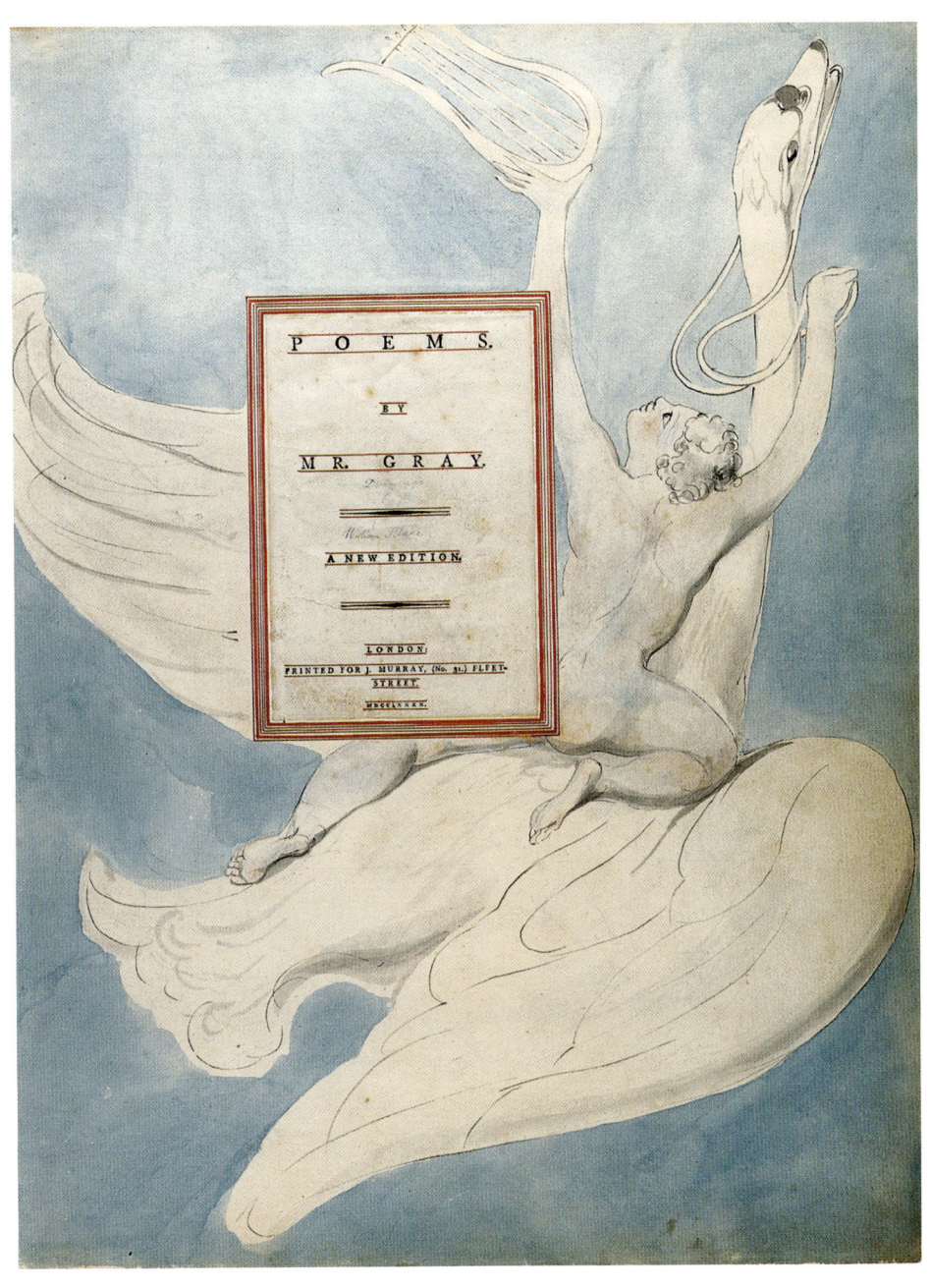

The Poems of Thomas Gray, Design 1,
"The Pindaric Genius Receiving His Lyre," pen and ink and watercolor

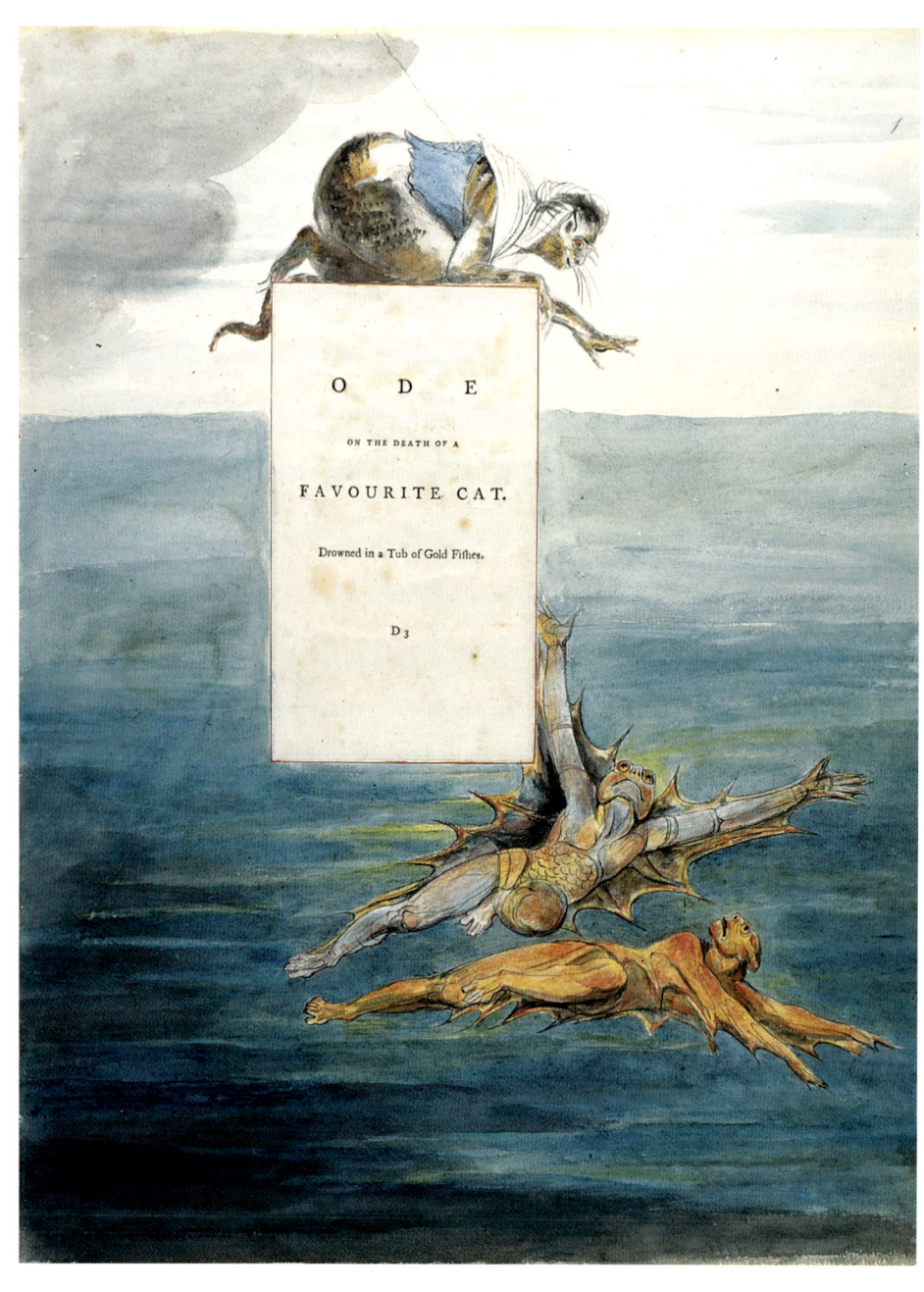

The Poems of Thomas Gray, Design 7,
"Ode on the Death of a Favorite Cat," pen and ink and watercolor

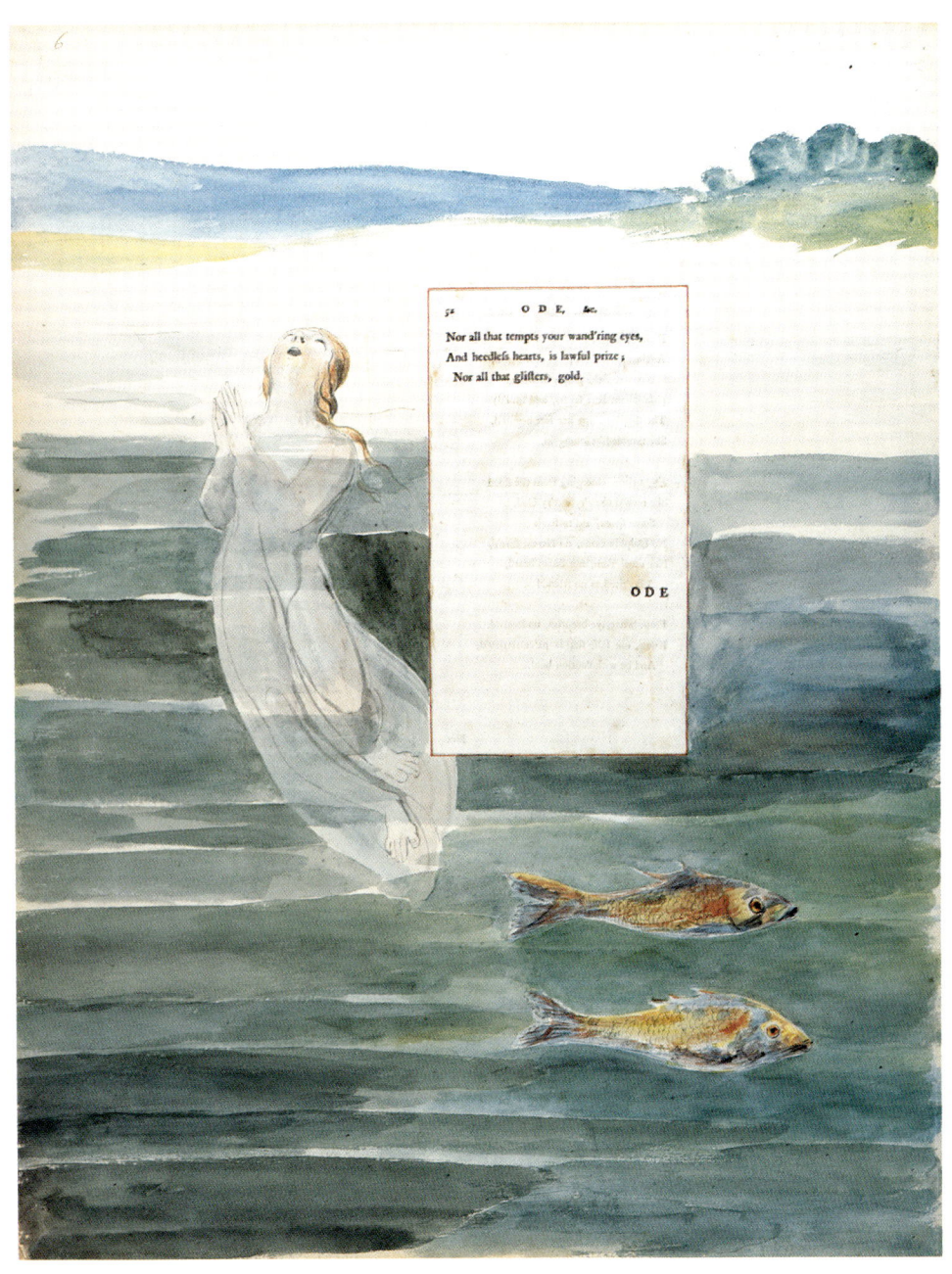

The Poems of Thomas Gray, Design 12,
"Ode on the Death of a Favorite Cat," pen and ink and watercolor

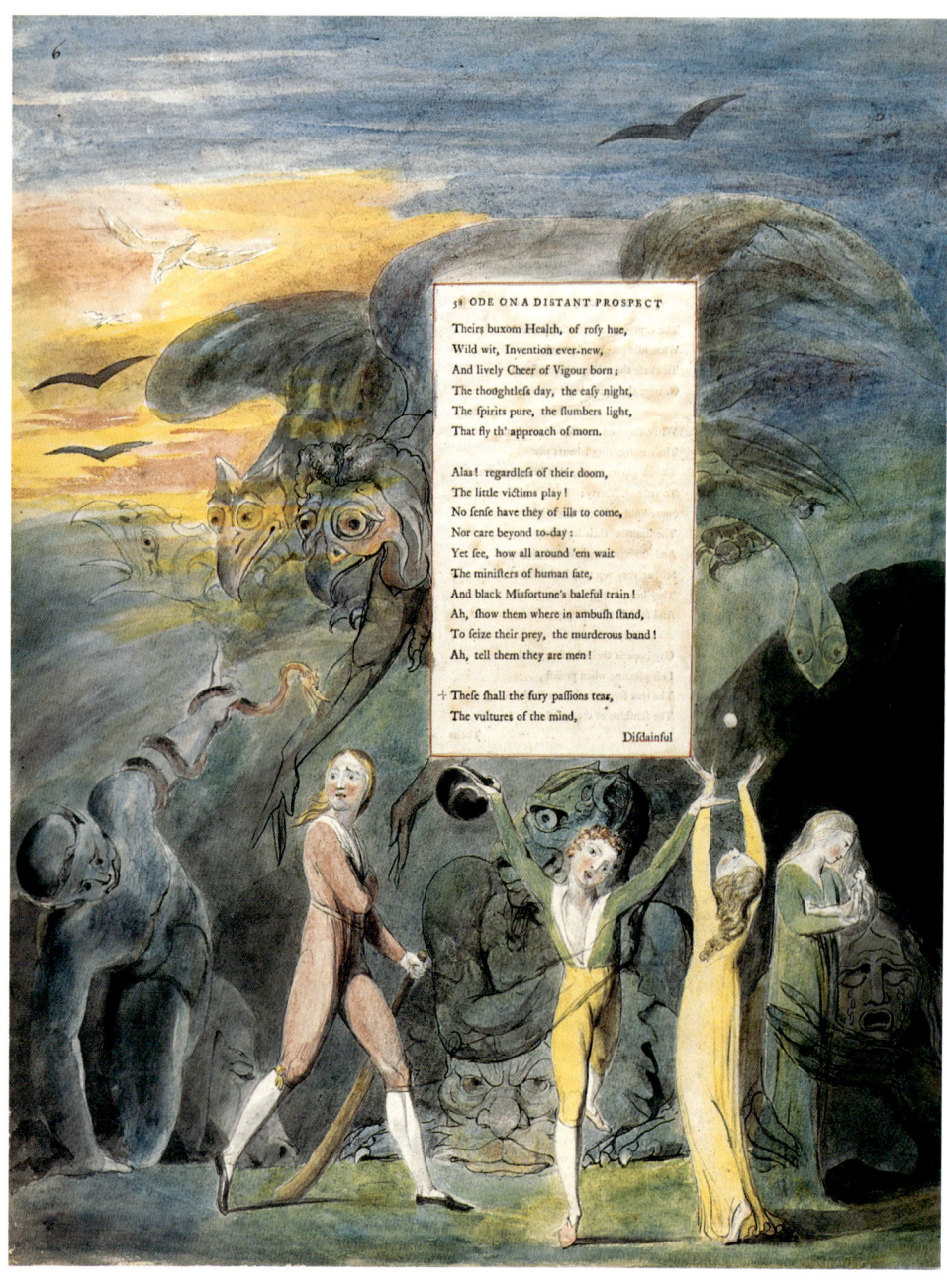

The Poems of Thomas Gray, Design 18,
"Ode on a Distant Prospect of Eton College," pen and ink and watercolor

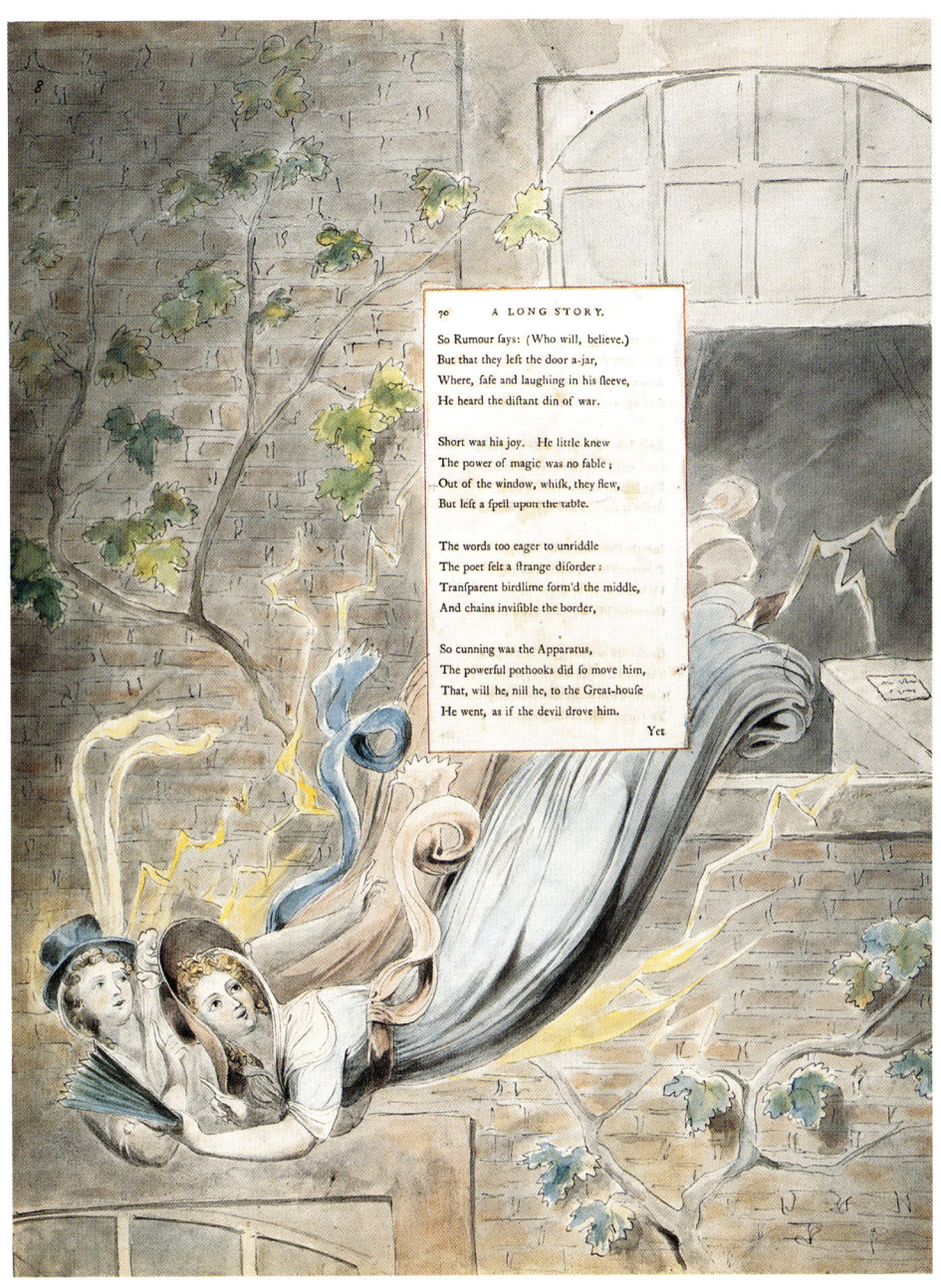

The Poems of Thomas Gray, Design 30,
"A Long Story," pen and ink and watercolor

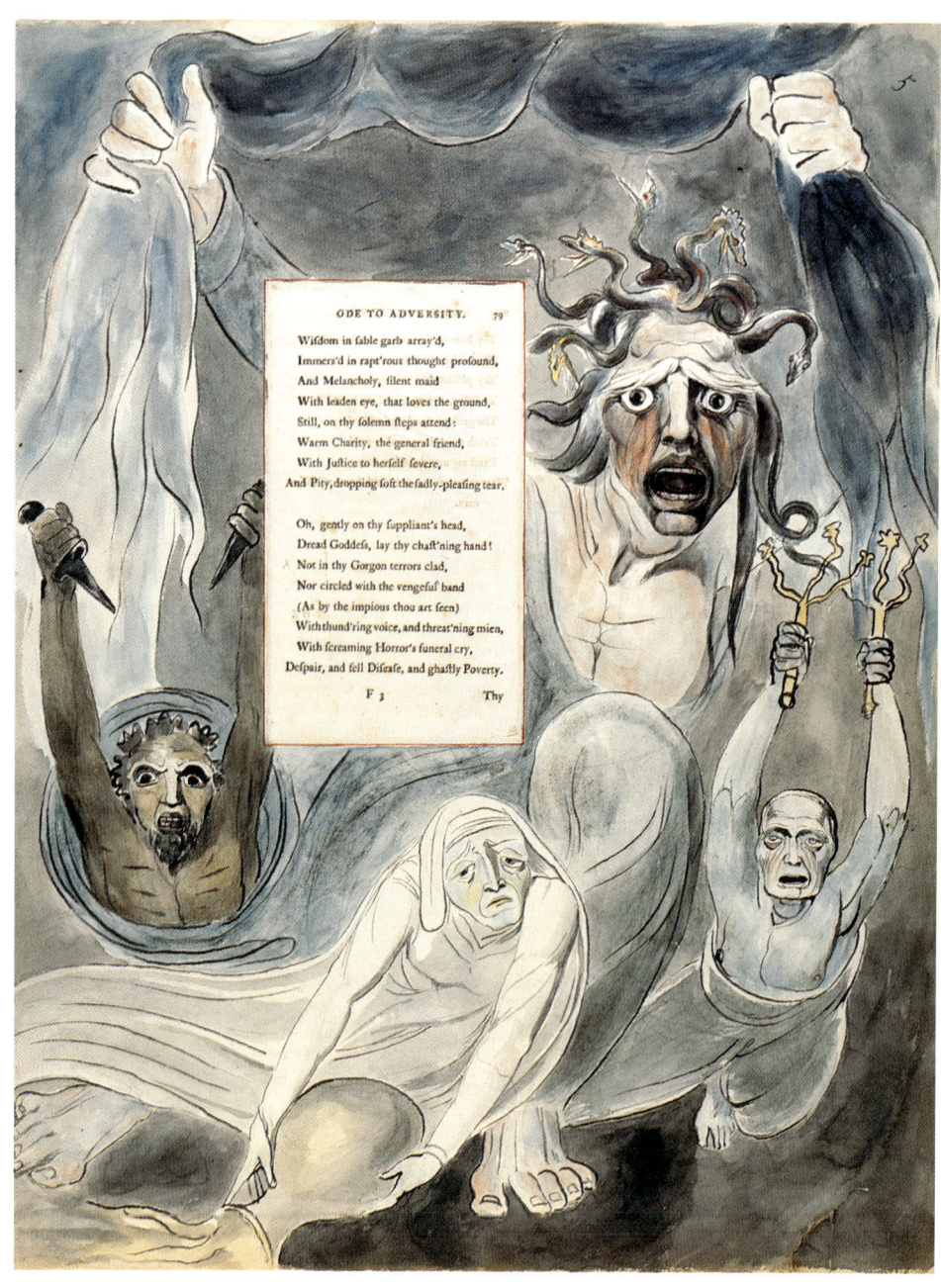

The Poems of Thomas Gray, Design 39,
"Ode to Adversity," pen and ink and watercolor

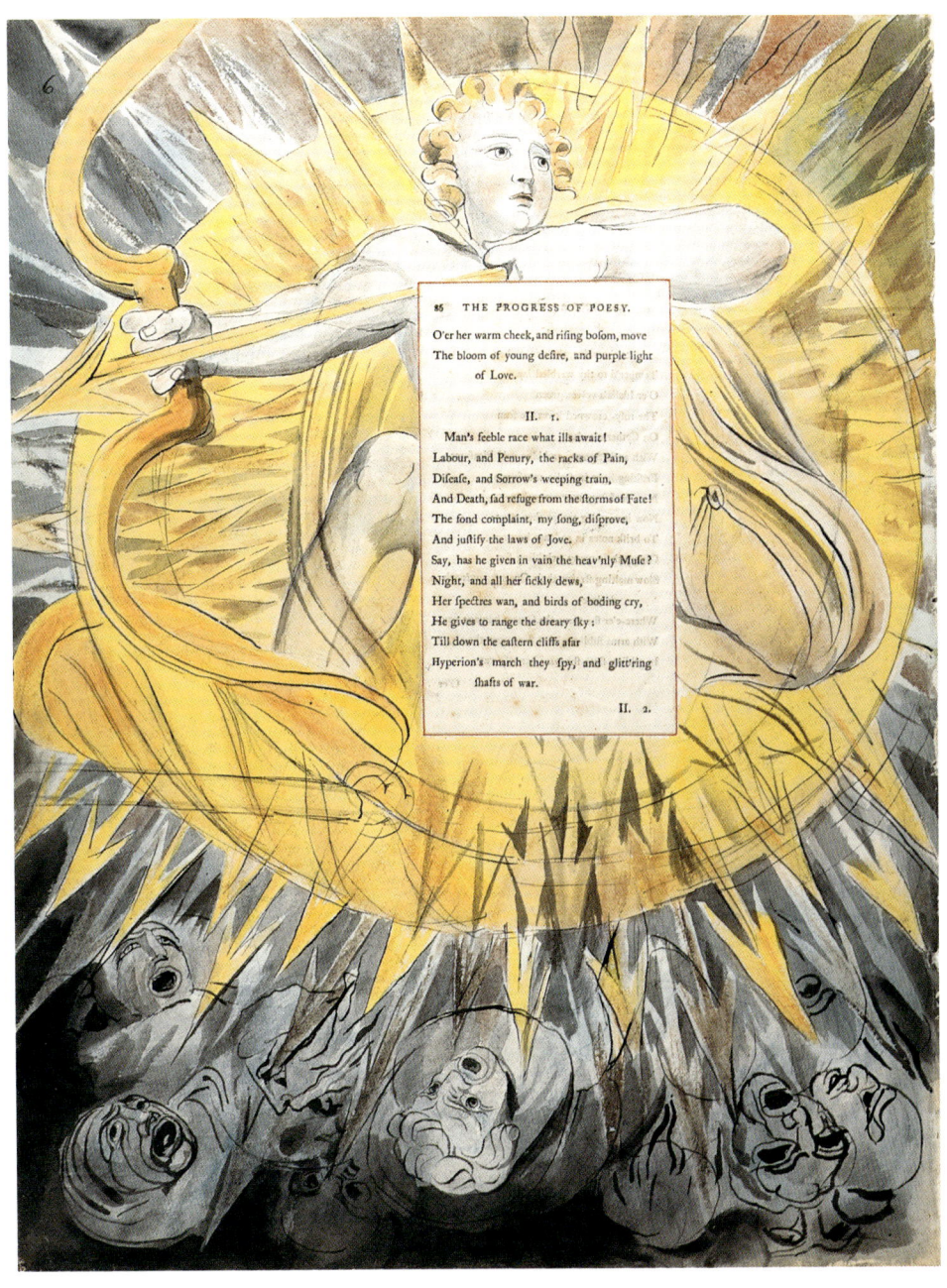

The Poems of Thomas Gray, Design 46,
"The Progress of Poesy. A Pindaric Ode," pen and ink and watercolor

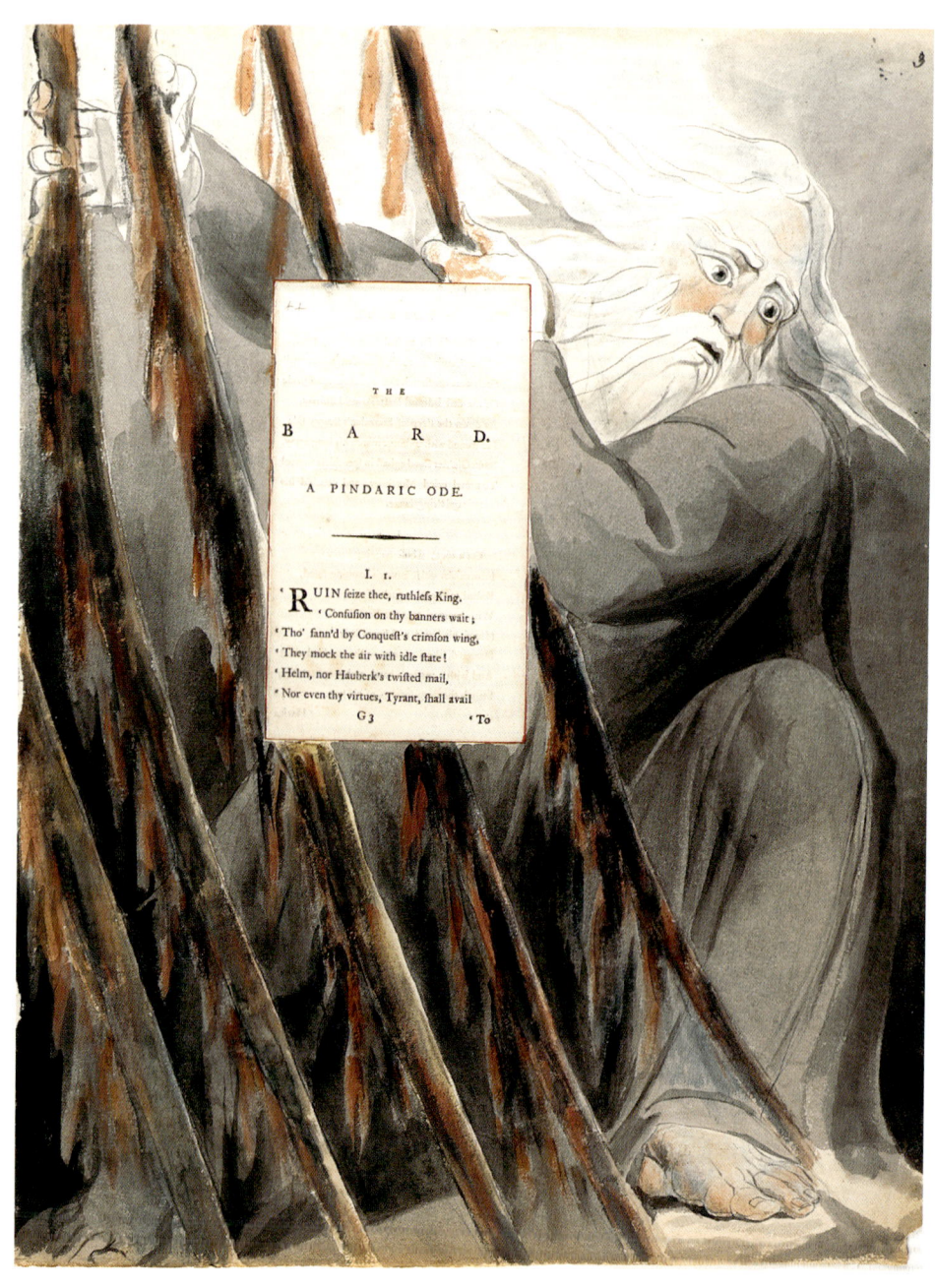

The Poems of Thomas Gray, Design 55,
"The Bard. A Pindaric Ode," pen and ink and watercolor

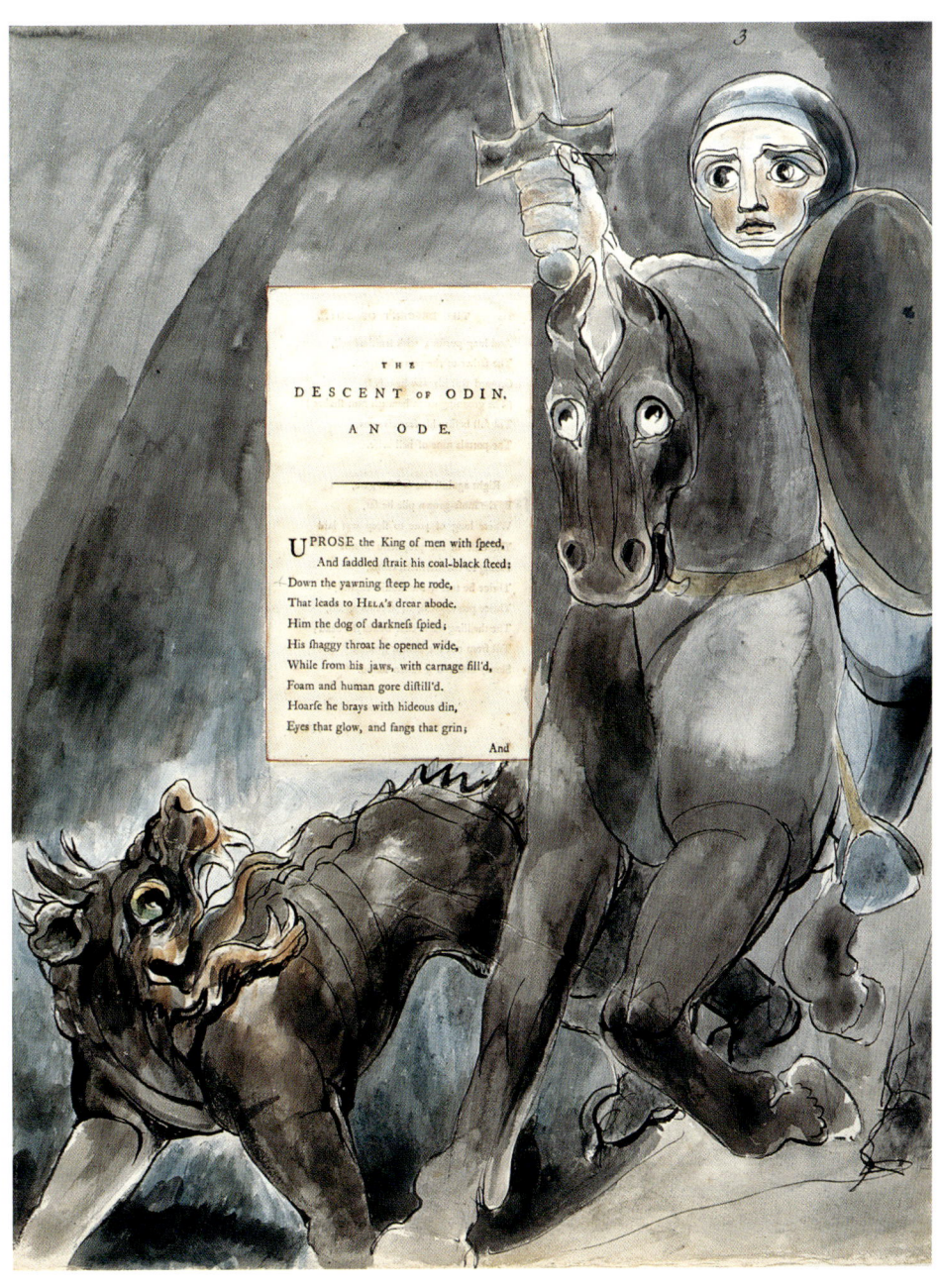

The Poems of Thomas Gray, Design 79,
"The Descent of Odin. An Ode," pen and ink and watercolor

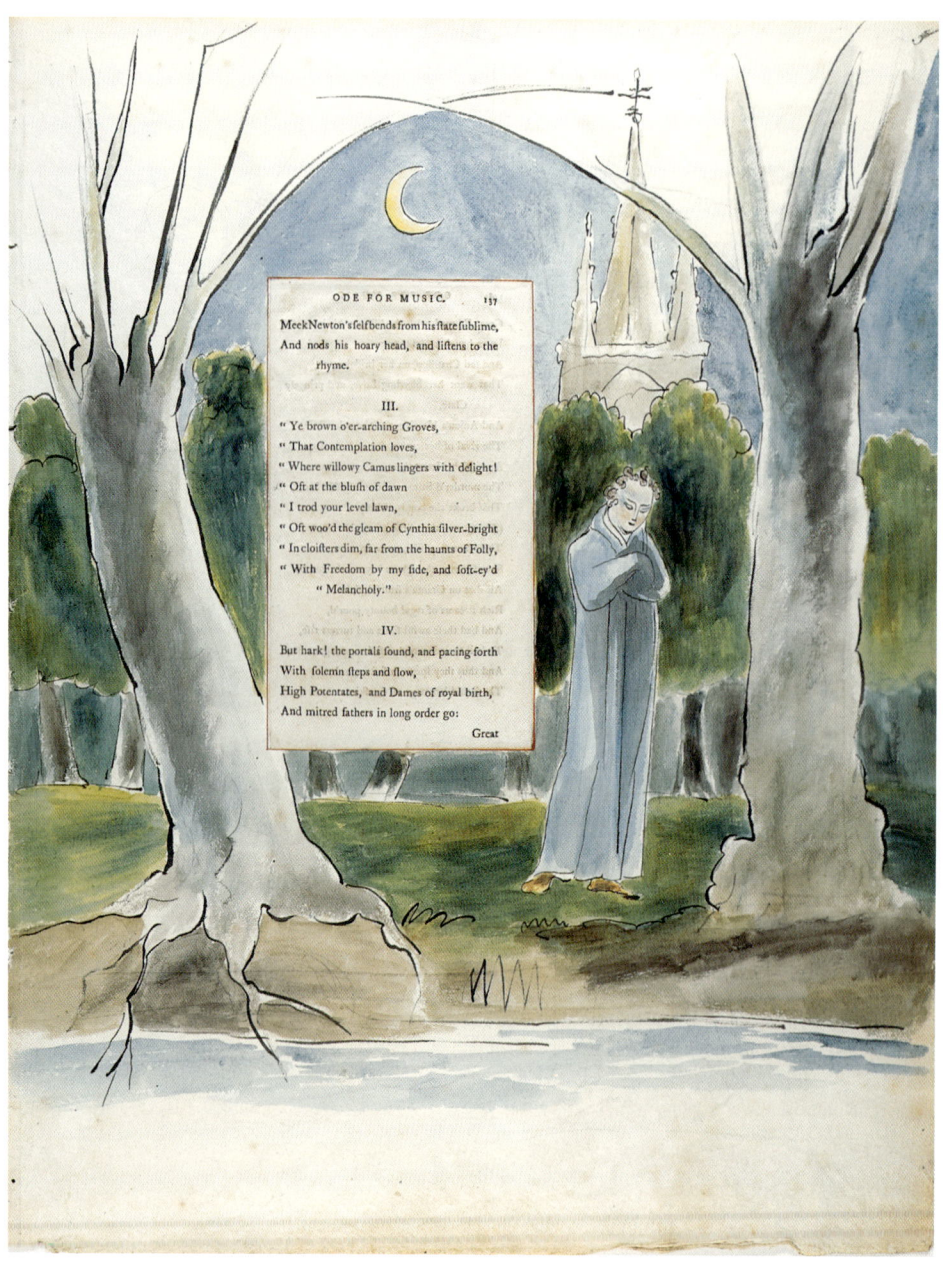

The Poems of Thomas Gray, Design 97,
"Ode for Music," pen and ink and watercolor

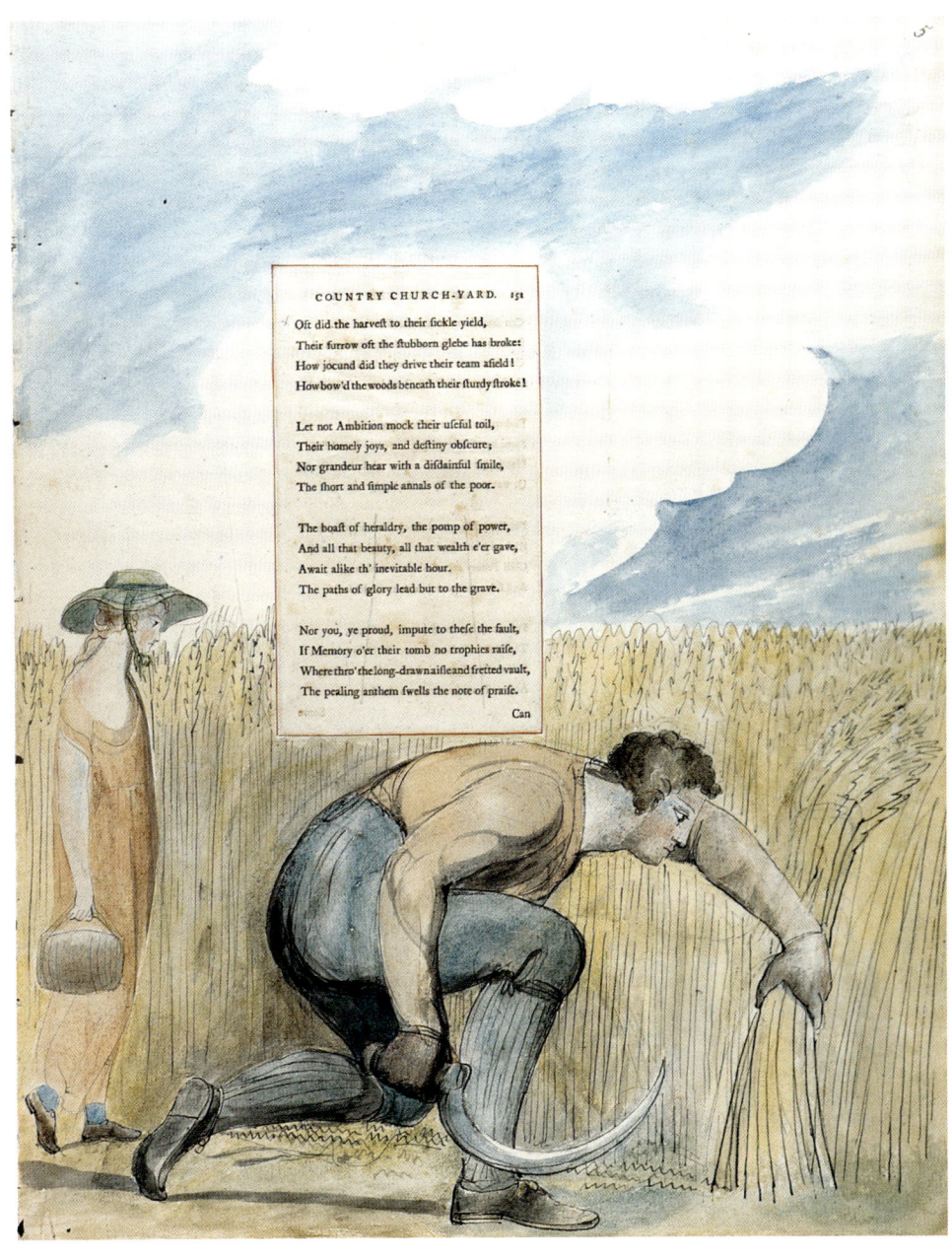

The Poems of Thomas Gray, Design 109,
"Elegy Written in a Country Church-Yard," pen and ink and watercolor

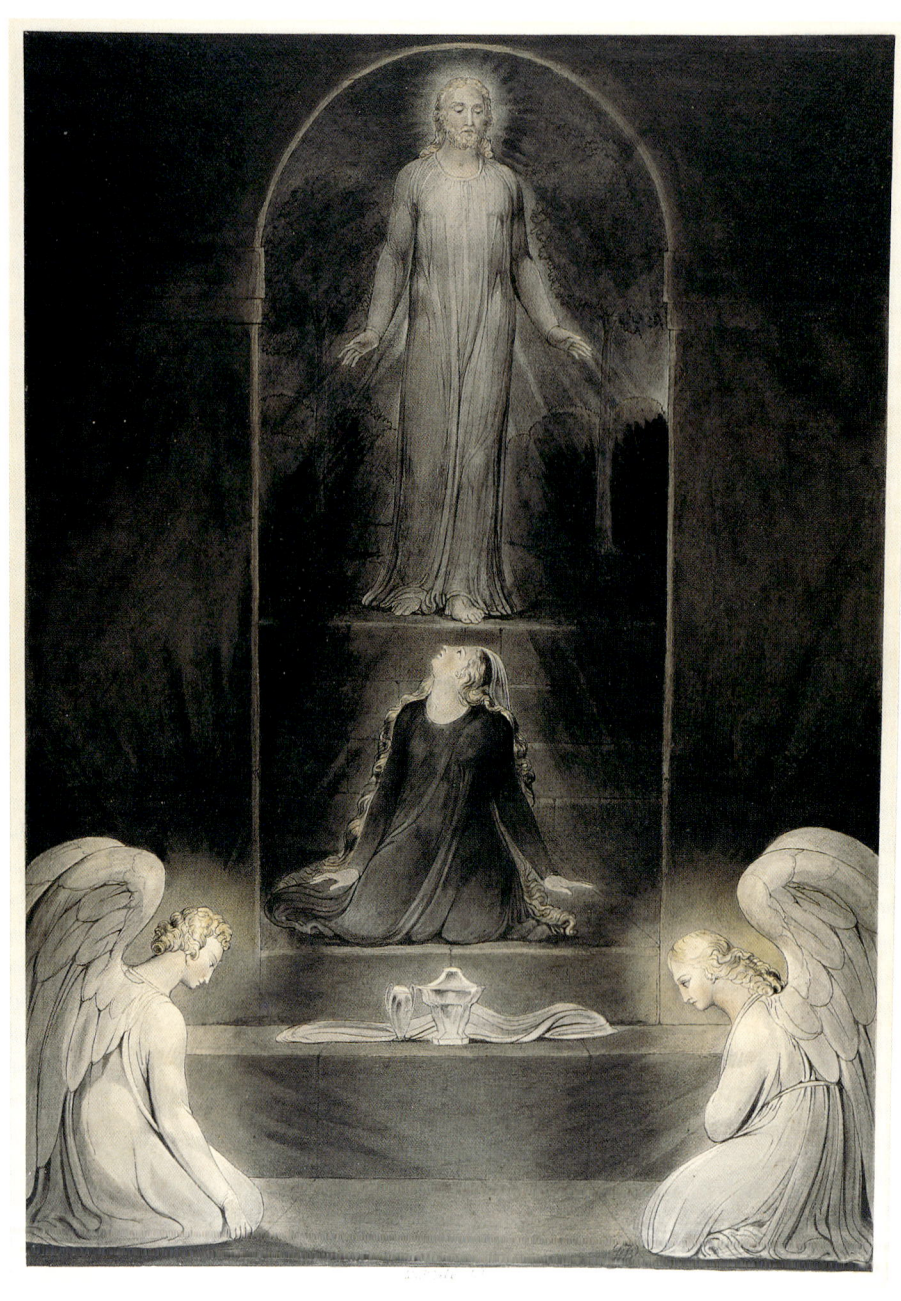

Mary Magdalen at the Sepulchre, pen and ink and watercolor

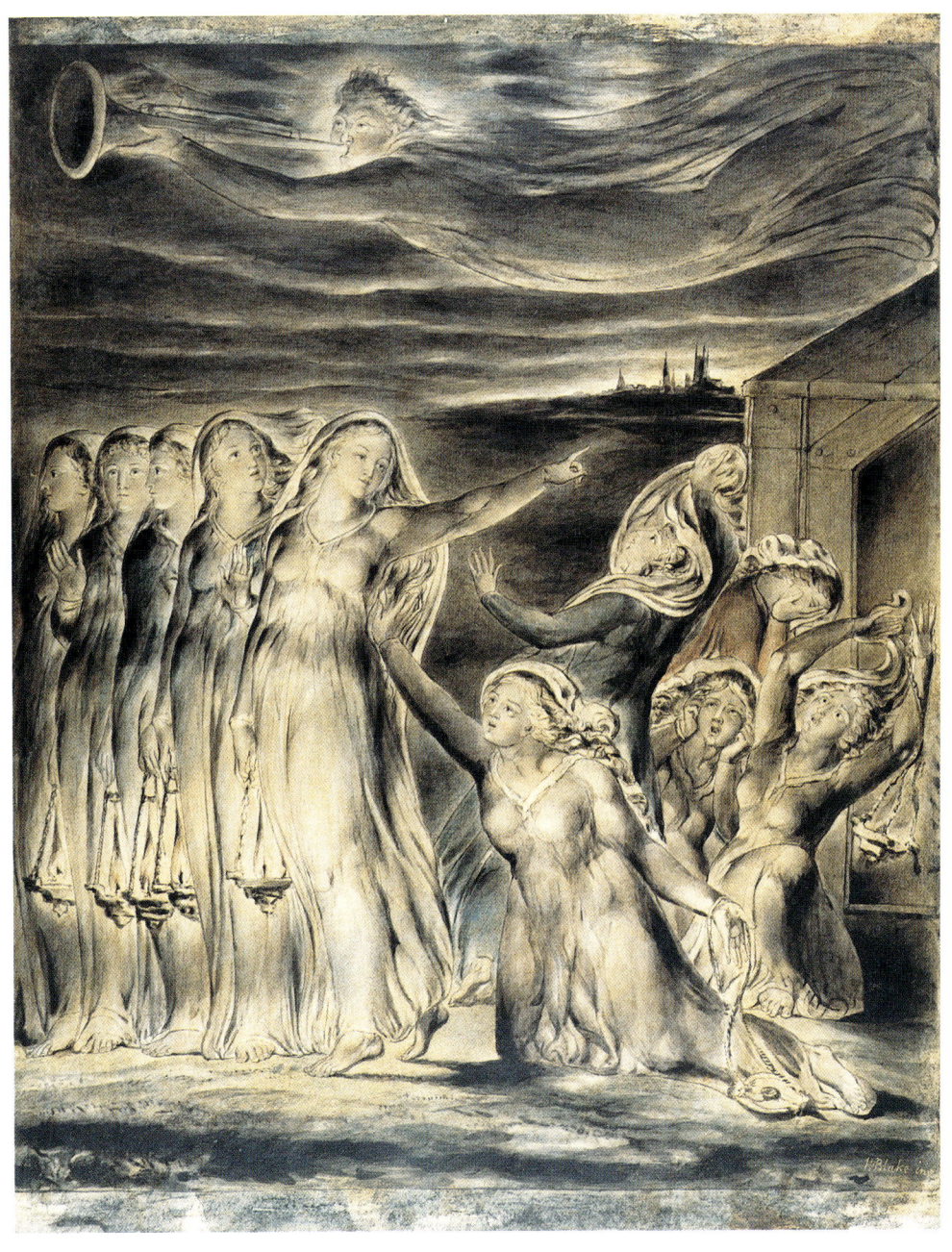

The Wise and Foolish Virgins, pen and ink and watercolor

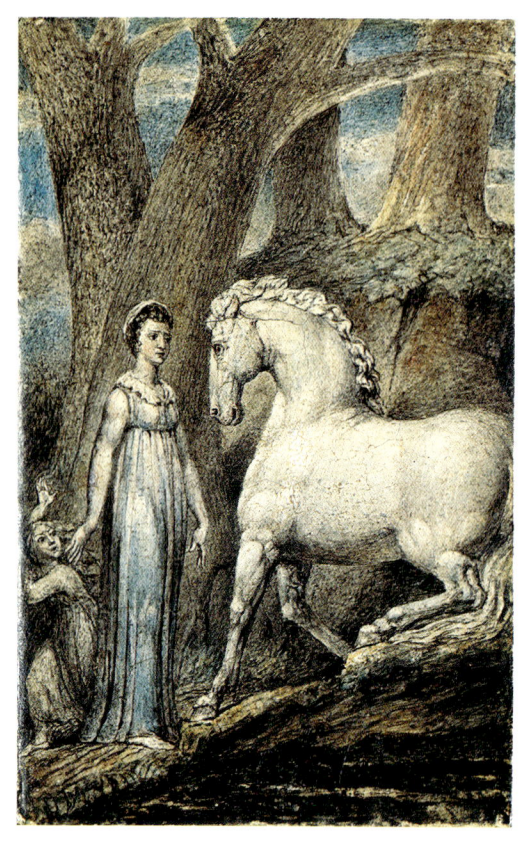

The Horse, tempera on copper

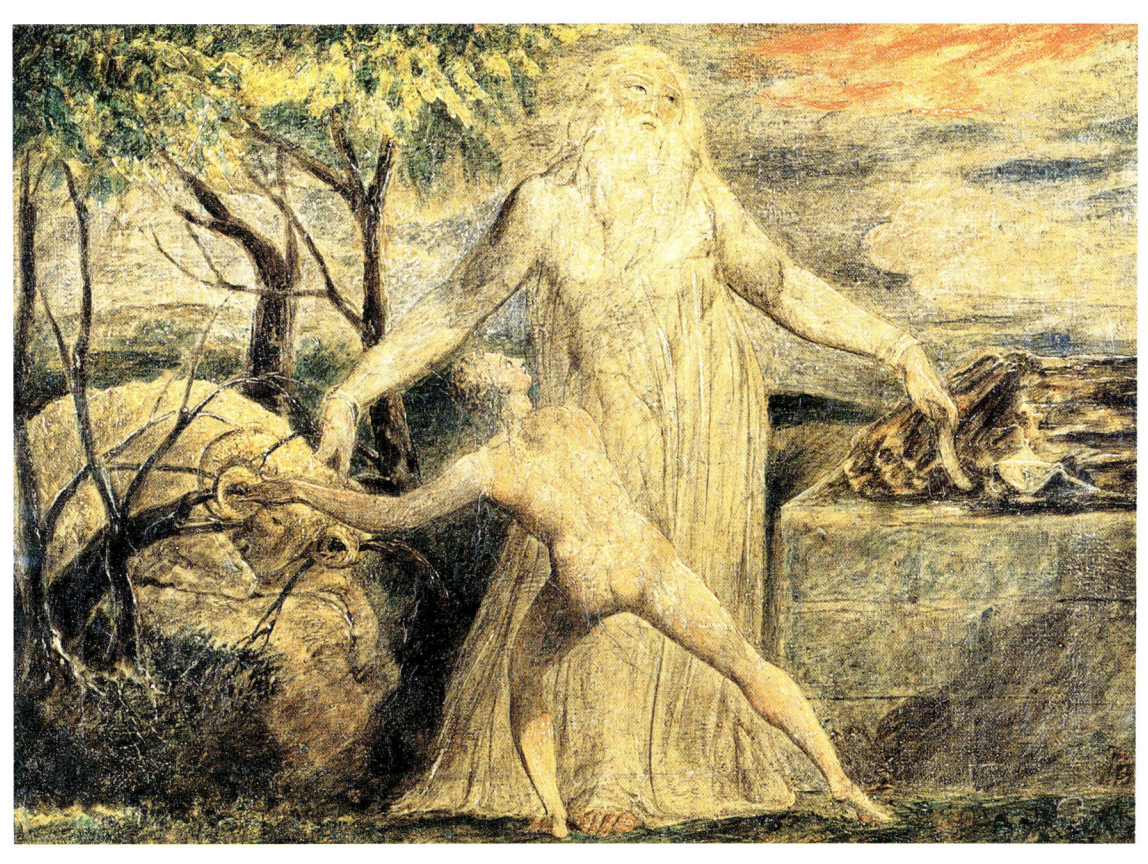

Abraham and Isaac, tempera

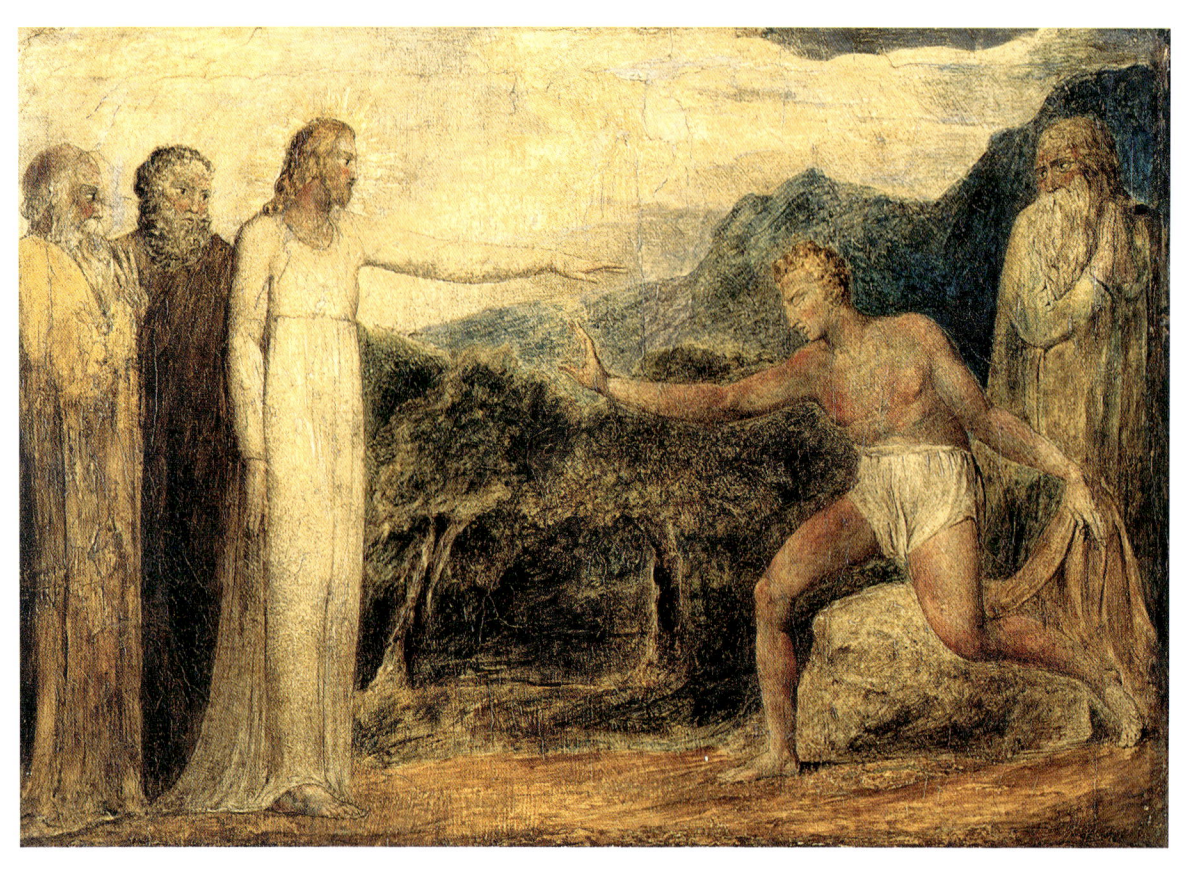

Giving Sight to Bartimaeus, tempera

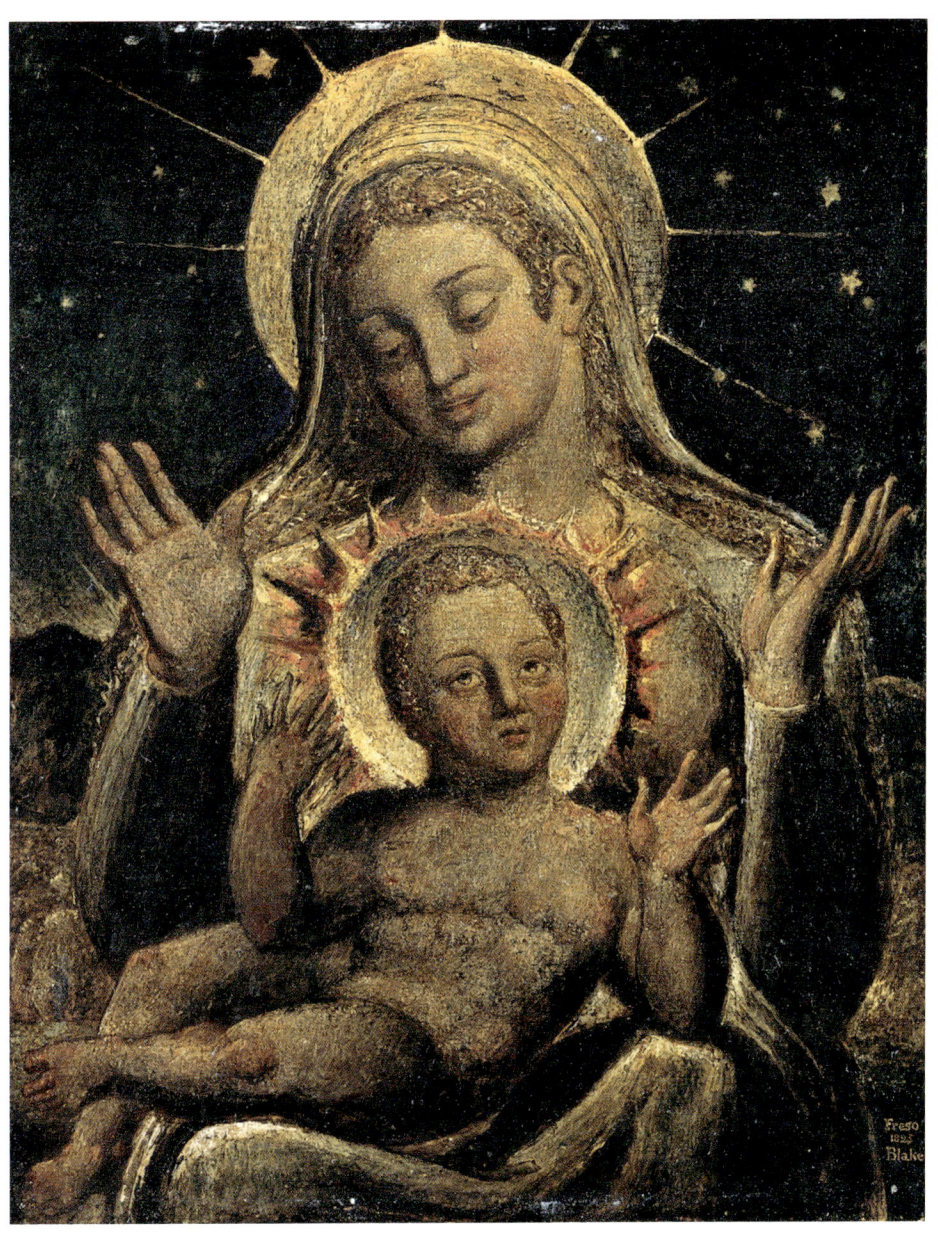

The Virgin and Child, tempera

CATALOGUE

CATALOGUE NOTE

The definitive modern studies of Blake's works in each media, to which I am indebted for much of the information offered in this publication, are cited in full in the References. Since the general bibliography of Blake is almost beyond human capacity to absorb in one lifetime, I have listed, in the Select Bibliography, only a handful of titles that are relevant to the specific works in the Mellon collection, or that have been helpful over the years or in the immediate compilation of this book. The checklist divides into the following sections: Illuminated Books, Temperas, Watercolors and Drawings, Prints, Illustrated Books, and Related Material. Within each category the works are listed chronologically. Although most of the catalogued works originated in the collection of Paul Mellon, this list also includes a few works by William Blake that were transferred permanently from the Yale University Art Gallery to the Yale Center for British Art in 1979, or that were given by other generous donors.

ILLUMINATED BOOKS

Blake first used the term "Illuminated Printing" in a prospectus of 1793 advertising his published illustrated poems. Beginning with *There Is No Natural Religion* in the late 1780s, he invented and later refined a unique autographic printmaking technique that enabled him to print both his text and designs from the same copper plates "in a style more ornamental, uniform, and grand than any before discovered." This technique, now referred to as "relief etching," involved painting and writing, in reverse, on the surface of the copper plate with an acid-resistant varnish. Acid was then poured over the plate to etch away the exposed areas and leave in relief the designs and text. Blake would then ink the raised areas and print the plate on paper using a standard engraver's rolling press. The earliest Illuminated Books were usually printed in one color of ink and then hand colored with watercolor. In about 1794, and for several years after that, Blake began printing the plates with a variety of thick colored inks in a process that resembles monotype. Although most of Blake's Illuminated Books have dated title pages, not all of the copies of any individual title were necessarily printed in the same year. Certain copies of the popular *Songs of Innocence and of Experience,* for instance, were printed as late as the 1820s. Joseph Viscomi's *Blake and the Idea of the Book* (Princeton, 1992) offers the most exhaustive study of Blake's process in creating the Illuminated Books. I have included Viscomi's dates for the printing of the Center's copies.

There Is No Natural Religion, c. 1788
 (printed c. 1794)

11 color-printed relief etchings, several touched with watercolor, on 11 leaves
SPINE: 5½ in. (14 cm); sheets: 5¼ × 4 in. (13.3 × 10.2 cm)
REFERENCES: Keynes and Wolf B; Bentley B
PROVENANCE: Possibly Frederick Tatham (1805–1878) (Sotheby's, 29 April 1862, lot 197, bt. Monckton Milnes); Richard Monckton Milnes, 1st Baron Houghton (1809–1885); his son, Richard Offley Ashburton Milnes, the Earl of Crewe (1858–1945) (Sotheby's, 30 March 1903, lot 10, bt. Quaritch); William A. White (1843–1927), from 1903; his daughter, Frances White Moffat, later Mrs. William Emerson, from 1927; (Thomas J. Gannon) from whom purchased by Paul Mellon, 1941.
B1992.2.15 (1–11)

Songs of Innocence, 1789

31 relief etchings printed in brown, with pen and ink and watercolor, on 17 leaves
DISBOUND SHEETS: 7⅝ × 5⅜ in. (19.4 × 13.2 cm)
REFERENCES: Keynes and Wolf G; Bentley G
PROVENANCE: Possibly anonymous (Puttick & Simpson's, 4 March 1872, lot 1,121); Anonymous (Sotheby's, 2 July 1895, lot 501, bt. Quaritch); William A. White (1843–1927); his daughter, Frances W. Moffat, later Mrs. William Emerson, from 1895 (Sotheby's, 19 May 1958, lot 2, bt. Stonehill for Paul Mellon).
B1992.8.12 (1–17)

Songs of Innocence, 1789
Songs of Experience, 1794

31 relief etchings printed in brown or green, with pen and ink and watercolor, on 17 leaves (*Innocence*); 17 color-printed relief etchings, with watercolor, on 17 leaves (*Experience*)
DISBOUND SHEETS: 7¼ × 4¾ in. (18.4 × 12.1 cm)

REFERENCES: Keynes and Wolf F; Bentley F
PROVENANCE: George Cumberland (1754–1848); Henry Burgess (Sotheby's, 17 April 1929, lot 583, bt. Walter T. Spencer); (Scribner's, 1938); Edison Dick; (Scribner's, 1947); (Thomas J. Gannon) through whom purchased by Paul Mellon, 1947.
B1978.43.1546–1579

Songs of Innocence and of Experience, 1789–1794 (printed 1795)
54 relief etchings printed in dark brown, with pen and ink and watercolor, on 54 leaves
SPINE: 7½ in. (9.1 cm); sheets: 7⅛ × 5 in. (8.1 × 12.7 cm)
REFERENCES: Keynes and Wolf L; Bentley L
PROVENANCE: Henry Little; Alfred G. Gray (Sotheby's, 15 December 1926, lot 613, bt. Walter T. Spencer); Cortlandt F. Bishop (1870–1935) (American Art Association–Anderson Galleries, 5 April 1938, lot 279); (Charles Sessler); Moncure Biddle (1882–1956); (Thomas J. Gannon) from whom purchased by Paul Mellon, 1948.
B1992.8.13(1–54)

Proof Impression of The Shepherd, from Songs of Innocence, 1789 (printed c. 1795)
Color-printed relief etching with watercolor
3 × 2¾ in. (7.6 × 6.9 cm)
REFERENCES: Butlin, no. 262A; Bentley, *Supplement*, p. 130
PROVENANCE: A Lady (Sotheby-Belgravia, 5 April 1977, lot 210, bt. Somerville and Simpson); (Somerville and Simpson) from whom purchased by Paul Mellon, 1977.
B1978.1.2

Proof Impression of Spring, from Songs of Innocence, 1789 (printed c. 1795)
Color-printed relief etching with watercolor
1⅞ × 2¾ in. (4.7 × 6.9 cm)
REFERENCES: Butlin, no. 262B; Bentley, *Supplement*, p. 130
PROVENANCE: A Lady (Sotheby-Belgravia, 5 April 1977, lot 209, bt. Somerville and Simpson); (Somerville and Simpson) from whom acquired by Paul Mellon, 1977.
B1978.1.1

The Book of Thel, 1789
8 relief etchings printed in brown, with pen and ink and watercolor, on 8 leaves
SPINE: 11⅝ in. (29.6 cm); sheets: 11⅜ × 9 in. (28.9 × 22.8 cm)
REFERENCES: Keynes and Wolf B; Bentley B
PROVENANCE: Richard Monckton Milnes, 1st Baron Houghton (1809–1885), by 1863; his son, Richard Offley Ashburton Milnes, the Earl of Crewe (1858–1945) (Sotheby's, 30 March 1903, lot 2, bt. Edwards); (Francis Edwards); Sir Algernon Methuen (1856–1924); his wife, Lady Methuen (Sotheby's, 19 February 1936, lot 501, bt. Quaritch for Philip Hofer); Philip Hofer (1898–1984), to 1949; (Thomas J. Gannon) from whom purchased by Paul Mellon, 1949.
B1992.8.3 (1–8)

The Book of Thel, 1789
8 relief etchings printed in brown, with pen and ink and watercolor, on 8 leaves in original paper wrappers
SPINE: 12 in. (30.4 cm); sheets: 12 × 9½ in. (30.4 × 24.1 cm)
REFERENCES: Keynes and Wolf R; Bentley R
PROVENANCE: H. A. Mair (Puttick & Simpson's, 19 November 1900, lot 339, bt. Quaritch); possibly Marsden Jasiel Perry (1850–1935) (American Art Association–Anderson Galleries, 11 March 1936, lot 37, bt. Drake); (James F. Drake) from whom purchased by a private collector; (James F. Drake, 1952); Hannah D. Rabinowitz; (C. A. Stonehill) from whom purchased by Paul Mellon, 1959.
B1978.43.1334–1341

Visions of the Daughters of Albion, 1793
11 relief etchings printed in green, with watercolor, on 6 leaves
SPINE: 14 in. (35.6 cm); sheets: 13⅝ × 9¾ in. (34.6 × 24.8 cm)
REFERENCES: Keynes and Wolf I; Bentley I
PROVENANCE: Possibly Sir William Tite (1798–1873) (Sotheby's, 19 May 1874, lot 293, bt. John Pearson); Thomas Gaisford (Sotheby's, 23 April 1890, lot 188, bt. Ellis); (Ellis & Elvey, to c. 1894); Anonymous (Hodgson's, 14 April 1904, lot 514, bt. Quaritch); (Bernard Quaritch) from whom purchased by William A. White (1843–1927), 1904; his niece, Mrs. Adrian Van Sinderen; (Thomas J. Gannon) from whom purchased by Paul Mellon, 1956.
B1978.43.1580–1585

America. A Prophecy, 1793 (printed c. 1807)
18 relief etchings printed in brown, blue, or black, with pen and ink and watercolor, some plates lightly color-printed, on 18 leaves
DISBOUND SHEETS: 14½ × 10½ in. (36.9 × 26.6 cm)
REFERENCES: Keynes and Wolf M; Bentley M

PROVENANCE: Richard Monckton Milnes, 1st Baron Houghton (1809–1885), by 1863; his son, Richard Offley Ashburton Milnes, the Earl of Crewe (1858–1945) (Sotheby's, 30 March 1903, lot 3, bt. Quaritch); William A. White (1843–1927), by 1905; his daughter, Frances W. Moffat, later Mrs. William Emerson (Sotheby's, 19 May 1958, lot 5, bt. Quaritch); (John F. Fleming) from whom purchased by Paul Mellon, 1958.
B1992.8.2 (1–18)

Europe. A Prophecy, 1793 (printed 1795)

17 relief etchings printed in dark brown, with watercolor and oil added posthumously, on 17 leaves

SPINE: 15 3/8 in. (39.1 cm); sheets: 15 1/4 × 10 5/8 in. (38.7 × 27 cm)

REFERENCES: Keynes and Wolf A; Bentley A
PROVENANCE: Probably George Romney (1734–1802); his son, John Romney (Christie's, 9 May 1834, lot 86+, bt. Tiffin); Isaac D'Israeli (1766–1848), from 1834; his son, Benjamin D'Israeli, Earl of Beaconsfield (1804–1881), who removed pl. 1–2, 4–6 by 1856, and sold pl. 7–18 (Sotheby's, 20 March 1882, lot 57, bt. James Bain); pl. 7–18 were with Bernard Buchanan MacGeorge (?1845–1924), by 1887; pl. 1–2, 4–6 sold by Anonymous (Hodgson's, 14 January 1904, lot 225, bt. Hopkins); plates reunited by Bernard Buchanan MacGeorge, by 1906 (Sotheby's, 1 July 1924, lot 116, bt. Wells); George C. Smith Jr. (1892–1937), by 1927 (Parke-Bernet, 2 November 1938, lot 26, bt. Sessler); Moncure Biddle (1882–1956), by 1939, by whom sold through (Thomas J. Gannon) to Paul Mellon, 1948.
B1992.8.4 (1–17)

The [First] Book of Urizen, 1794

28 color-printed relief etchings, with watercolor, on 28 leaves

SPINE: 10 1/4 in. (26 cm); sheets: 10 × 7 1/8 in. (25.4 × 18.1 cm)

REFERENCES: Keynes and Wolf A; Bentley A
PROVENANCE: Possibly 1st Baron Dimsdale (1712–1800); by descent to Maj. T. E. Dimsdale (Sotheby's, 28 February 1956, lot 531, bt. Samuel); Howard Samuel, to 1958; (John F. Fleming) from whom purchased by Paul Mellon, 1958.
B1992.8.5 (1–28)

The [First] Book of Urizen, 1794

26 color-printed relief etchings, with watercolor, on 26 leaves

DISBOUND SHEETS: 11 7/8 × 9 5/8 in. (30.2 × 24.3 cm)

REFERENCES: Keynes and Wolf C; Bentley C
PROVENANCE: (John Pearson, by 1854); Thomas Gaisford (Sotheby's, 23 April 1890, lot 191, bt. Nugent); Britwell Court Library; by descent to Maj. S. V. Christie-Miller (Sotheby's, 29 March 1971, lot 35, bt. Wynne Jeudwine); (John Baskett) from whom purchased by Paul Mellon, 1972.
B1978.43.1419–1444

Jerusalem, c. 1804–1820 (printed c. 1821)

100 relief etchings printed in orange-brown, with pen and ink and watercolor, some plates touched with gold, on 100 leaves

DISBOUND SHEETS: 13 1/2 × 10 3/8 in. (34.3 × 26.4 cm)

REFERENCES: Keynes and Wolf E; Bentley E
PROVENANCE: Probably Catherine Blake (1761–1831); Frederick Tatham (1805–1878), from c. 1831; George Blamire (?1788–1863) (Christie's, 6 November 1863, lot 213, bt. Daniels); William Fuller Maitland (1813–1876), to 1876; Anonymous (Christie's, 1 June 1887, lot 225, bt. Quaritch); (Bernard Quaritch) from whom purchased by Gen. Archibald Stirling of Keir, c. 1893; his son, Col. William Stirling, by whom sold through (Scribner's, 1952) to Paul Mellon.
B1992.8.1 (1–100)

Proof Impressions, on one sheet, of Jerusalem, Plate 28 (recto) and Plate 35 (verso), c. 1820

Relief etchings with pen and ink and watercolor
12 1/2 × 9 3/8 in. (31.7 × 23.8 cm)

REFERENCE: Bentley, p. 263
PROVENANCE: Possibly H. E. Scudder, 1880; possibly William A. White, by 1905; A. S. W. Rosenbach, to 1952; Hannah D. Rabinowitz, from 1952 to 1970; (C. A. Stonehill) from whom purchased by Paul Mellon, 1970.
B1992.8.1 (105)

Proof Impressions, on one sheet, of Jerusalem, Plate 30 (recto) and Europe, Frontispiece (verso), c. 1820

Relief etchings, the recto with pen and ink and watercolor
12 1/2 × 9 3/8 in. (31.7 × 23.8 cm)

REFERENCE: Bentley, p. 161
PROVENANCE: Possibly A. Macmillan, 1876; possibly William A. White, by 1905; A. S. W. Rosenbach, by 1939 to 1952; Hannah D. Rabinowitz, from 1952 to 1970; (C. A. Stonehill) from whom purchased by Paul Mellon, 1970.
B1992.8.1 (106)

TEMPERAS

Tempera is the term that most nearly describes Blake's improvised medium—a mixture of whiting and carpenter's glue applied in multiple thin layers to a canvas or copper support and then painted on with pigments suspended in a similar glue binder. He chose glue as a binder because he considered the gum arabic normally favored in watercolors less durable. The generous use of pen and ink assured a desired clarity of form and detail, and a final application of glue size consolidated the delicate surface.

Abraham and Isaac, c. 1799–1800
Tempera with pen and black ink on canvas
10¼ × 14¾ in. (26 × 37.5 cm)
REFERENCE: Butlin, no. 382
PROVENANCE: Thomas Butts (1759–1845); Thomas Butts Jr.; Capt. F. J. Butts; his widow, by whom sold through Carfax Gallery in 1906 to Walford Graham Robertson (1866–1948) (Christie's, 22 July 1949, lot 3, bt. Clifton); Mrs. A. B. Clifton, from whom purchased by Paul Mellon, 1961.
B1977.14.89

Christ Giving Sight to Bartimaeus, c. 1799–1800
Tempera with pen and black ink on canvas
10¼ × 14¾ in. (26 × 37.5 cm)
REFERENCE: Butlin, no. 420
PROVENANCE: Thomas Butts (1759–1845); Thomas Butts Jr. (Foster's, 29 June 1853, lot 85, as *Restoring Sight to the Blind,* with lots 86–87, bt. Strange); Henry Willet (née Catt) (Christie's, 10 April 1905, lot 2 as *Christ Healing the Leper,* bt. Carfax); (Carfax Gallery); Mrs. A. B. Clifton, from whom purchased by Paul Mellon, 1961.
B1977.14.90

The Horse, from William Hayley's Ballads, c. 1805–1806
Tempera with pen and black ink on a copper engraving plate
4³⁄₁₆ × 2½ in. (10.6 × 6.2 cm)
REFERENCE: Butlin, no. 366
PROVENANCE: George Blamire (?1788–1863) (Christie's, 7 November 1863, lot 138, bt. Bohn); Henry George Bohn; Upholland College, Wigan (Christie's, 27 October 1961, lot 43, bt. Colnaghi's); (P. & D. Colnaghi) from whom purchased by Paul Mellon, 1962.
Collection of Mr. and Mrs. Paul Mellon

The Virgin and Child ("The Black Madonna"), c. 1825
Tempera and gold on panel
11¼ × 9¼ in. (28.5 × 23.5 cm)
REFERENCE: Butlin, no. 674
PROVENANCE: George Blamire (?1788–1863) (Christie's, 7 November 1863, lot 3, bt. Daniel); Alexander Anderdon Weston, by 1876; (Carfax Gallery, 1906); A. B. Clifton; Mrs. A. B. Clifton by 1934, from whom purchased by Paul Mellon, 1961.
B1977.14.91

WATERCOLORS AND DRAWINGS

Moses Receiving the Law, c. 1780
Brush and black ink over graphite
25¹⁵⁄₁₆ × 12¼ in. (65.9 × 31.1 cm)
REFERENCE: Butlin, no. 111
PROVENANCE: Catherine Blake (1761–1831); Frederick Tatham (1805–1878) (Sotheby's, 29 April 1862, lot 167, with 3 others, bt. Palser); possibly Lt. Col. Francis Cunningham (Sotheby's, 11 May 1876, lot 650, bt. Thompson); Theodore Lucas, by 1906; Iolo A. Williams, from whom purchased through (P. & D. Colnaghi) by Paul Mellon, 1966.
B1975.4.1883

Satan Approaching the Court of Chaos, c. 1784–1785
Graphite, pen and brown ink, and grey wash; verso: graphite sketch of the same composition
9¼ × 13¼ in. (23.6 × 33.6 cm)
REFERENCE: Butlin, no. 102 (where dated c. 1780)
PROVENANCE: Possibly Catherine Blake (1761–1831); possibly Frederick Tatham (1805–1878) (Sotheby's 29 April 1862, lot 174, subject unspecified, with 7 others, bt. Weston); Col. Gould Weston: Mrs. Hunter-Weston; Miss Nora Hunter (Christie's, 15 July 1957, lot 19, bt. Agnew's); (Thomas J. Agnew) from whom purchased in 1958 by Lady Melchett (Christie's, 9 November 1971, lot 78, bt. Baskett and Day for Paul Mellon).
B1975.4.1459

Tiriel Supporting the Dying Myratana and Cursing His Sons, c. 1786–1789
Pen and brush and black ink
7⁵⁄₁₆ × 10¹¹⁄₁₆ in. (18.6 × 27.2 cm)
REFERENCE: Butlin, no. 198/1
PROVENANCE: Possibly Catherine Blake (1761–1831); possibly Frederick Tatham (1805–1878) from whom

purchased by Joseph Hogarth (Southgate's, 8 June 1854, lot 643, as *Twelve Elaborate Subjects, Designed to Illustrate a Work, the Subject Unknown*, bt. Morley); Elhanan Bicknell (Christie's, 1 May 1863, lot 387, bt. Leathart); James Leathart (d. 1896); Percival W. Leathart, by 1906; Mrs. Leathart, by 1957 (Sotheby's, 19 May 1958, lot 13, bt. Baskett and Day for Paul Mellon).
B1977.14.4150

Illustrations to Thomas Gray's Poems, c. 1797–1798
116 watercolors with pen and black ink, on 58 leaves
DISBOUND SHEETS: 16½ × 12¾ in. (41.9 × 32.4 cm)
REFERENCE: Butlin, no. 335
PROVENANCE: Ann Flaxman (née Denman, d. 1820), 1798; her husband, John Flaxman (1755–1826) (Christie's, 1 July 1828, lot 85, bt. Clarke for William Beckford); William Beckford (1760–1844); his daughter, Susan, Duchess of Hamilton, and by descent to Sir Douglas Douglas-Hamilton (1903–1973), 14th Duke of Hamilton, from whom purchased by Paul Mellon, 1966.
B1992.8.11 (1–58)

Thomas Alphonso Hayley, Half-Length Drawing, c. 1800
Graphite and sepia wash
6¾ × 5³⁄₁₆ in. (17.2 × 13.2 cm)
REFERENCE: Butlin, no. 345
PROVENANCE: Possibly Catherine Blake (1761–1831); possibly Frederick Tatham (1805–1878) (Sotheby's, 29 April 1862, lot 178, bt. Ford); (Quaritch, to 1864); George A. Smith (Christie's, 1 April 1880, lot 168, bt. Quaritch); Bernard Buchanan MacGeorge (?1845–1924) by 1912 (Sotheby's, 1 July 1924, lot 133, bt. Parsons); (Maggs, 1924); George C. Smith Jr. (1892–1937) (Parke-Bernet, 2 November 1938, lot 97, bt. Sessler); Charles Rosenbloom, by whom given to Yale University Art Gallery, 1972; transferred to the Yale Center for British Art, 1979.
B1979.12.741

Sealing the Stone and Setting a Watch, c. 1800–1803
Pen and grey ink and watercolor over graphite
16 × 13⅛ in. (40.1 × 33.3 cm)
REFERENCE: Butlin, no. 499
PROVENANCE: Thomas Butts (1759–1845); Thomas Butts Jr.; Capt. F. J. Butts (Sotheby's, 24 June 1903, lot 16, bt. in); his widow by whom sold through Carfax Gallery in 1906 to Walford Graham Robertson (1866–1948) (Christie's, 22 July 1949, lot 36, bt. Meatyard); (Meatyard, to 1954); (C. A. Stonehill) from whom purchased by Yale University Art Gallery, 1956; transferred to the Yale Center for British Art, 1979.
B1979.12.703

The Entrance Front of Hayley's House at Eartham, 1801
Pen and black ink and watercolor over graphite
5⅜ × 9 (13.6 × 22.7)
REFERENCE: Butlin, no. 369
PROVENANCE: Catherine Blake (1761–1831); Frederick Tatham (1805–1878); (Bernard Quaritch, by 1882) from whom purchased in 1886 by Walford Graham Robertson (1866–1948) (Christie's, 22 July 1949, lot 80a, bt. Agnew's); L. G. Duke, by whom sold in 1953 to Colnaghi's; Richard Delano, by whom sold to Wildenstein's, by 1964; (d'Offay Couper Gallery, 1968); John Torson, 1968; (Anthony d'Offay Gallery, 1978); (Miss Yvonne ffrench) from whom purchased by Paul Mellon, 1978.
B1981.25.2396

Landscape with a Spire, c. 1801
Graphite
6¹⁄₁₆ × 8¹³⁄₁₆ in. (15.4 × 22.4 cm)
REFERENCE: Butlin, no. 371
PROVENANCE: Catherine Blake (1761–1831); Frederick Tatham (1805–1878); (Bernard Quaritch, by 1882) from whom purchased in 1886 by Walford Graham Robertson (1866–1948) (Christie's, 22 July 1949, lot 80b, bt. Agnew's); L. G. Duke, by whom sold to Colnaghi's, 1952; (P. & D. Colnaghi) from whom purchased by Paul Mellon, 1961.
B1977.14.4922

A Woody Landscape, c. 1801
Watercolor and graphite
5⅞ × 9 in. (15 × 22.9 cm)
REFERENCE: Butlin, no. 372
PROVENANCE: Catherine Blake (1761–1831); Frederick Tatham (1805–1878); (Bernard Quaritch, by 1882) from whom purchased in 1886 by Walford Graham Robertson (1866–1948) (Christie's, 22 July 1949, lot 80, bt. Agnew's); L. G. Duke, by whom sold to Colnaghi's, 1952; (P. & D. Colnaghi) from whom purchased by Paul Mellon, 1961.
B1977.14.4923

Joseph and Potiphar's Wife, c. 1803–1805
Pen and black ink and watercolor
14 × 12¾ in. (35.5 × 32.3 cm)

REFERENCE: Butlin, no. 439
PROVENANCE: Thomas Butts (1759–1845), Thomas Butts Jr. (Sotheby's, 26 March 1852, lot 186, bt. Bohn); Henry George Bohn; (Robson & Co., 1904); Walford Graham Robertson (1866–1948), from 1904 (Christie's, 22 July 1949, lot 5, bt. Fine Art Society); (C. A. Stonehill, 1949); Hannah D. Rabinowitz, from 1950 to 1974; (Charles Traylen) from whom purchased by Paul Mellon, 1974.
B1977.14.4309

Albion Compelling the Four Zoas to Their Proper Tasks, c. 1804–1810

Graphite

9⅞ × 12¼ in. (25 × 31.2 cm)

REFERENCE: Butlin, no. 571
PROVENANCE: E. J. Shaw (Sotheby's, 29 July 1925, lot 145, bt. Kaye); Frederick Benjamin Kaye, presented in his memory by Warren H. Lowenhaupt to Yale University, 1930; transferred to Yale Center for British Art, 1979.
B1979.12.718

Mary Magdalen at the Sepulchre, c. 1805

Watercolor and pen and black ink

16¹³⁄₁₆ × 12¼ in. (42.7 × 31.1 cm)

REFERENCE: Butlin, no. 504
PROVENANCE: Thomas Butts (1759–1846); Thomas Butts Jr. (Sotheby's, 26 March 1852, lot 155, bt. Palgrave); F. T. Palgrave, by whom given to Lady Beatrix Maud Cecil on the occasion of her marriage in 1883 to William Waldegrave Palmer, 2nd Earl of Selborne, to 1950; (Walker's Galleries, 1950); (Thomas J. Agnew, 1951), from whom purchased by Capt. and Mrs. V. Bulkeley-Johnson (the Mount Trust), February 1951 (Christie's, 5 June 1973, lot 42, bt. Agnew); (Thomas J. Agnew) from whom purchased by Paul Mellon, 1973.
B1975.4.1794

The Widow Embracing Her Husband's Grave, c. 1805–1808

Pen and brush and black ink and watercolor

6¹⁄₁₆ × 8³⁄₁₆ in. (15.4 × 20.8 cm)

REFERENCE: Butlin, no. 633
PROVENANCE: Possibly Joseph Hogarth (Southgate's, 7 June 1854, lot 237, as *Children at the Grave of Their Parent,* with 4 others, bt. Palser); J. F. Hall, by 1876; (Carfax Gallery); Mrs. Louisa Bishop, née Salaman, by 1912; her son, Euston Bishop (Sotheby's, 19 May 1958, lot 11, bt. Agnew's for Melchett); Lady Melchett (Christie's, 9 November 1971, lot 74, bt. Baskett and Day for Paul Mellon).
B1975.1026

The Gambols of Ghosts According with Their Affections Previous to the Final Judgement (?), c. 1805–1808

Graphite and brown wash

18⅛ × 12⁷⁄₁₆ in. (46 × 31.6 cm)

REFERENCE: Butlin, no. 636
PROVENANCE: Catherine Blake (1761–1831); Frederick Tatham (1805–1878) (Sotheby's, 29 April 1862, lot 165 or 167, bt. Palser); Alfred Aspland, by 1876 (Sotheby's, 27 June 1885, lot 65, bt. Ogden); Mrs. Charles Hill; her heirs, from whom purchased through (Somerville and Simpson) by Paul Mellon, 1977.
B1978.18

An Angel with a Trumpet, c. 1805–1808

Pen and black ink and watercolor

7 13⁄16 × 4⁵⁄₁₆ in. (19.8 × 10.4 cm)

REFERENCE: Butlin, no. 611
PROVENANCE: Thomas Butts (1759–1845); Thomas Butts Jr., and by descent (Sotheby's, 22 March 1910, lot 447, bt. Robson); Anonymous (Sotheby's, 16 February 1949, lot 16, bt. Duke); L. G. Duke (Sotheby's, 29 April 1971, lot 12, bt. Baskett for Paul Mellon).
B1975.4.44

Copy of the Laocoön, for Rees's Cyclopaedia, 1815

Graphite

12⅝ × 8 15⁄₁₆ in. (32 × 22.8 cm)

REFERENCE: Butlin, no. 679
PROVENANCE: Catherine Blake (1761–1831); Frederick Tatham (1805–1878); Alfred Aspland, by 1876 (Sotheby's, 27 January 1885, lot 66, bt. Ogden of Oxford); G. Arkwright by whom sold through (Robson, 1905) to Walford Graham Robertson (1866–1948) (Christie's, 22 July 1949, lot 67, bt. Sawyer); (Philip C. Duschnes, to 1959); Henry J. Crocker (Parke-Bernet, 14 March 1963, lot 193, bt. Lane); Dr. Frederick Zimann (Lane Corporation), to 1985; (Thomas Galdy) from whom purchased by the Yale Center for British Art, 1985.
B1985.14

A Visionary Head, c. 1819–1820

Graphite; verso: graphite sketch of a monument

7½ × 5½ in. (19 × 14.2 cm)

REFERENCE: Butlin, no. 759
PROVENANCE: Catherine Blake (1761–1831); Frederick

Tatham (1805–1878); (Bernard Quaritch, by 1882) from whom purchased in 1886 by Walford Graham Robertson (1866–1948) (Christie's, 22 July 1949, lot 63, bt. Maggs); Mrs. John McCarthy (née Lambert), by whom given to Paul Mellon, 1963.
B1975.4.43

Five Visionary Heads of Women, c. 1819–1820

Graphite

10⅝ × 12¾ in. (28.6 × 32.4 cm)

REFERENCE: Butlin, no. 765

PROVENANCE: Mrs. Alexander Gilchrist, by 1863; H. H. Gilchrist (Sotheby's, 24 June 1903, lot 28, bt. Tregaskis); Julius Edwards, by whom sold to Colnaghi's, 1964; (P. & D. Colnaghi) from whom purchased by Paul Mellon, 1964.
B1975.4.1025

Socrates, c. 1820

Graphite

8⅝ × 7¼ in. (22.5 × 18.5 cm)

REFERENCE: Butlin, no. 714

PROVENANCE: John Varley (1778–1842); Albert Varley; Alfred Aspland (Sotheby's, 27 January 1885, lot 69, bt. Odgen of Oxford); G. Arkwright, by whom sold through (Robson's, 1905) to Walford Graham Robertson (1866–1948) (Christie's, 22 July 1949, lot 59, bt. Agnew's); Anonymous (Sotheby's, 23 May 1962, lot 20, bt. Colnaghi's for Paul Mellon).
B1975.4.42

Study for a Destroying Deity, c. 1820–1825

Graphite

17¹¹⁄₁₆ × 21 in. (45 × 61 cm)

REFERENCE: cf. Butlin, no. 778

PROVENANCE: Thomas E. Lowinsky; his son Justin Lowinsky, from whom acquired by Paul Mellon, 1963.
B1977.14.6079

The Parable of the Wise and Foolish Virgins, c. 1825

Watercolor and pen and black ink

16⅝ × 13⅞ in. (42.2 × 35.3 cm)

REFERENCE: Butlin, no. 480

PROVENANCE: William Haines (1778–1848); his granddaughter Miss Haines; J. Edwards (Sotheby's, 20 December 1938, lot 456, bought in and sold to Stonehill and Colnaghi); Gabriel Wells (1862–1946); Alfred Edward Newton (1864–1940) (Parke-Bernet 16 April 1941, lot 117, bt. Gannon); (Thomas J. Gannon) from whom purchased by Paul Mellon, 1941.
B1977.14.6102

PRINTS

For Children. The Gates of Paradise, 1793

18 etchings with engraving, on 18 leaves, in a contemporary paper binding

SPINE: 5⅝ in. (4.3 cm); sheets: 5⅜ × 4½ in. (13.6 × 11.4 cm)

REFERENCE: Bentley E

PROVENANCE: John Henry Fuseli (1741–1825), by whom given on 22 November 1806 to Harriet Jane Moore (b. 1801) (granddaughter of John Moore, physician to the Lockes of Norbury Park); her sister, Julia Moore (1803–1904); bequeathed to her cousin, George Heath (d. 1926); Mrs. M. C. Heath (Sotheby's, 4 April 1949, lot 75D, bt. Raphael King); (C. A. Stonehill) from whom purchased by Paul Mellon, 1949.
B1978.43.1484–1501

Pity, c. 1795

Color print with pen and black ink and watercolor, varnished

16⅜ × 20³⁄₁₆ in. (41.6 × 51.3 cm)

REFERENCE: Butlin, no. 312

PROVENANCE: Possibly Catherine Blake (1761–1831); possibly Frederick Tatham (1805–1878); possibly Joseph Hogarth, by c. 1843, when offered through George Richmond to John Ruskin; possibly Arthur Burgess (d. 1887), by 1878 to 1880; J. W. Pease, to 1901; by descent to Miss S. H. Pease; her executor, Lord Wardington (Christie's, 2 December 1938, lot 56, bt. in); Lady Wardington and by descent (Sotheby's, 28 November 1974, lot 137, bt. in); (Colin Franklin) from whom purchased by Paul Mellon, 1977.
B1977.14.6321

Christ Appearing to the Apostles after the Resurrection, c. 1795–1805

Color print with watercolor and pen and black ink, varnished

17 × 22½ in. (43 × 57.3 cm)

REFERENCE: Butlin, no. 325

PROVENANCE: Thomas Butts (1759–1845); Thomas Butts, Jr.; J. C. Strange, by 1863; possibly Harvey, by c. 1865; possibly the Rev. Samuel Price (Sotheby's, 11 December 1865, lot 275, as *The Resurrection*, bt. Halstead); Johnson, from whom purchased by Charles Eliot Norton, 1867 (American Art Association Gal-

leries, 2 May 1923, lot 13, bt. Wells); Gabriel Wells (1862–1946) from whom purchased by Yale University Art Gallery, 1929; transferred to Yale Center for British Art, 1979.
B1979.12.1039

Rev. John Caspar Lavater, 1787–1801
Engraving, third state
14 3/8 × 11 5/8 in. (36.5 × 29.6 cm)
REFERENCE: Essick, *Separate Plates,* no. XXIX (3U)
B1970.3.484

The Beggar's Opera, Act III, c. 1790
Engraving
17 7/16 × 22 9/16 in. (44.3 × 59.8 cm)
REFERENCE: Essick, *Separate Plates,* no. LXI
B1978.43.911

EDWARD YOUNG (1683–1765)
The Complaint and the Consolation: or Night Thoughts, London, 1797
43 engravings
SPINE: 16 3/4 in. (42.5 cm); sheets: 16 1/2 × 12 3/4 in. (41.9 × 32.3 cm)
REFERENCE: Bentley, *Supplement,* p. 270
PROVENANCE: Claude Edmund Delbos
B1978.43.1342–1379

EDWARD YOUNG (1683–1765)
The Complaint and the Consolation: or Night Thoughts, London, 1797
43 hand-colored engravings (with a notation by William Ensom "This copy was coloured/for me by Mr. Blake")
SPINE: 16 3/4 in. (42.5 cm); sheets: 16 1/2 × 12 7/8 in. (41.9 × 32.7 cm)
REFERENCE: Bentley Q
PROVENANCE: Probably William Ensom (1796–1832); Earl Spencer; possibly Anonymous (Hodgson's, 2 July 1914, lot 528, bt. Dobell); a Lady in Geneva (Sotheby's, 3 March 1958, lot 47, bt. Traylen and Stonehill for Paul Mellon).
B1978.43.1380–1417

EDWARD YOUNG (1683–1765)
The Complaint or the Consolation: or Night Thoughts, London, 1797
41 hand-colored engravings and prospectus (with a letter by Chauncey Tinker asserting that the coloring is Blake's)

SPINE: 16 3/4 in. (42.5 cm); sheets: 16 1/2 × 13 in. (42 × 33 cm)
REFERENCE: Bentley N
PROVENANCE: Alfred Edward Newton (1864–1940), by 1936 (Parke-Bernet, New York, 16–18 April 1941, lot 138, bt. Sessler); Wilmarth Sheldon Lewis (1895–1979), by whom given to Paul Mellon, 1967.
B1992.8.10 (1–41)

Chaucer's Canterbury Pilgrims, c. 1810–1820
Engraving, third state
13 3/4 × 37 5/8 in. (34.9 × 95.6 cm)
REFERENCE: Essick, *Separate Plates,* no. XVI (3X)
PROVENANCE: (Christopher Mendez) from whom purchased by Paul Mellon, 1971.
B1977.14.11092

The Man Sweeping the Interpreter's Parlour, c. 1822
White-line metal cut
7 × 9 1/8 in. (17.8 × 23.2 cm)
REFERENCE: Essick, *Separate Plates,* no. XX (2N)
PROVENANCE: Greville Macdonald, by 1913 to 1927; (Francis Edwards, 1927) from whom purchased by Ruthven Todd (Sotheby's, 11 December 1973, lot 25, bt. Tunick); (David Tunick) (Christie's, 4 July 1979, lot 173, bt. Baskett and Day for Paul Mellon).
B1981.25.769

Illustrations of the Book of Job, 1825
22 engravings on wove paper
SPINE: 16 1/2 in. (40.2 cm); sheets: 15 × 10 3/4 in. (38 × 27.3 cm)
REFERENCES: Bindman, nos. 625–646; Bentley 421
PROVENANCE: Alfred Edward Newton (1864–1940) (Parke-Bernet, 16 April 1941, bt. Gannon for Paul Mellon).
B1978.43.1502–1523

Illustrations of the Book of Job, 1825
22 engravings on india proof paper
SPINE: 17 1/4 in. (43.8 cm); sheets: 17 × 12 3/4 in. (43 × 32.5 cm)
REFERENCES: Bindman, nos. 625–646; Bentley 421
PROVENANCE: Mrs. F. S. Cameron-Head, Inverailort Castle, from whom purchased by Paul Mellon, 1971.
B1978.43.1524–1542

For the Sexes: The Gates of Paradise, c. 1826
20 engravings on wove paper with watermarks "J Whatman/1826"

SPINE: 13¾ in. (34.9 cm); sheets: 13⅜ × 9⅜ in. (34 × 23.8 cm)
REFERENCE: Bentley G
PROVENANCE: Possibly George Blamire (?1788–1863) (Christie's, 7–9 November 1863); James, 9th Earl of Southesk (1827–1905), by 1864; (Bernard Quaritch); (Sotheby's, 19 October 1954, lot 279, bt. Stonehill); (C. A. Stonehill) from whom purchased by Paul Mellon, 1955.
B1992.8.6 (1–20)

Illustrations to Dante's Divine Comedy, 1827
7 engravings on india proof paper
DISBOUND SHEETS: 10⅝ × 13¹⁵⁄₁₆ in. (27 × 35.4 cm)
REFERENCES: Bindman, nos. 647–653; Bentley 448
PROVENANCE: (P. & D. Colnaghi) from whom purchased by Paul Mellon, 1962.
B1992.8.8 (1–7)

Illustrations to Dante's Divine Comedy, 1827
7 engravings on india proof paper
SPINE: 22¼ in. (56.5 cm); sheets: 22 × 15¾ in. (55.8 × 40 cm)
REFERENCES: Bindman, nos. 647–653; Bentley 448
PROVENANCE: Philip Hofer (1898–1984); (Robert M. Light) from whom purchased by Paul Mellon, 1960.
B1992.8.9 (1–7)

ILLUSTRATED BOOKS WITH ENGRAVINGS BY OR AFTER BLAKE

JAMES STUART (1713–1788) and NICHOLAS REVETT (1720–1804)
The Antiquities of Athens, London, 1762–1794
REFERENCE: Essick, *Commercial*, no. XXVIII
T127.6 (f°)

SIR JOSEPH AYLOFFE (1709–1781)
An Account of Some Ancient Monuments in Westminster Abbey, in *Vetusta Monumenta*, vol. 2, London, 1780
7 engravings without text
REFERENCE: Easson and Essick, no. XVI
B1977.14.16519–16522, 16524, 16526, 16528

FRANCIS BLACKBURNE (1705–1787)
Memoirs of Thomas Hollis, London, 1780
REFERENCE: Essick, *Commercial*, appendix i, D
CT788/H74/+B6/1780

HENRY EMLYN (1728/9–1815)
A Proposition for a New Order in Architecture, London, 1781
REFERENCE: Essick, *Commercial*, no. IV
L15.3 (f°)

JOSEPH RITSON (1752–1803)
A Select Collection of English Songs, London, 1783
REFERENCE: Essick, *Commercial*, no. XIV
B1978.43.1694–1709

RICHARD GOUGH (1735–1801)
Sepulchral Monuments in Great Britain, London, 1786
REFERENCE: Essick, *Commercial*, appendix i, F
Folio A/N/130

JOHN GAY (1685–1732)
Fables, London, 1793
REFERENCE: Essick, *Commercial*, no. XXVI
PROVENANCE: Gift of Kenneth D. Rapoport, M.D.
B1982.22.1–2

GEORGE CUMBERLAND (1754–1848)
Thoughts on Outline, Sculpture, and the System that Guided the Ancient Artists, London, 1796
REFERENCE: Essick, *Commercial*, no. XXXII
B1978.43.1603–1626 and 1627–1649 (2 copies)

JOHN GABRIEL STEDMAN (1744–1797)
Narrative, of a Five Years' Expedition, Against the Revolted Negroes of Surinam, London, 1796
REFERENCE: Essick, *Commercial*, no. XXXIII
F2410/+S81/1796/2 copies

The Monthly Magazine, and British Register, London, October 1797
REFERENCE: Essick, *Commercial*, no. XXXV
Serials (8°) 17

WILLIAM HAYLEY (1745–1820)
An Essay on Sculpture in a Series of Epistles to John Flaxman, London, 1800
REFERENCE: Essick, *Commercial*, no. XXXIX [a detached impression of Essick XXXIX(3) *Thomas Hayley* is also in the collections: no. B1977.14.12366]
B1978.43.1650–1652

CHRISTIAN GOTTHILF SALZMANN (1744–1811)
Gymnastics for Youth, London, 1800

REFERENCE: Essick, *Commercial*, appendix ii, no. 17
B1978.43.1710–1719

HENRY FUSELI (1741–1825)
Lectures on Painting, London, 1801
REFERENCE: Essick, *Commercial*, no. XL
ND1150/+F9/2 copies

WILLIAM HAYLEY (1745–1820)
The Life, and Posthumous Writings, of William Cowper, London, 1803–1804
REFERENCE: Essick, *Commercial*, no. XLIV
B1978.43.1653–1672

WILLIAM HAYLEY (1745–1820)
The Triumphs of Temper, London, 1803
REFERENCE: Essick, *Commercial*, no. XLIII
B1978.43.1685–1690

WILLIAM HAYLEY (1745–1820)
Ballads, London, 1805
REFERENCE: Essick and Easson VIII
B1978.8 (a–e)

BENJAMIN HEATH MALKIN (1769–1842)
A Father's Memoirs of His Child, London, 1806
REFERENCE: Essick, *Separate Plates*, no. LVI
B1978.43.1691–1693

ROBERT BLAIR (1699–1746)
The Grave. A Poem, London, 1808
REFERENCE: Bindman, nos. 465–476
PROVENANCE: Alsop; (H. D. Lyon) from whom purchased by Paul Mellon, 1966.
B1978.43.1445–1457; 1458–1470/2 copies

ROBERT BLAIR (1699–1746)
The Grave. A Poem, London, 1808
Frontispiece and 12 engravings without text in portfolio
REFERENCE: Bindman, nos. 465–476
PROVENANCE: (B. Weinreb) from whom purchased by Paul Mellon, 1966.
B1978.43.1471–1483

WILLIAM HAYLEY (1745–1820)
The Life of George Romney, Chichester, 1809
REFERENCE: Essick, *Commercial*, no. XLIX
B1978.43.1673–1684

JOHANN CASPAR LAVATER (1741–1801)
Essays on Physiognomy, London, 1810
REFERENCE: Essick, *Commercial*, no. XIX
L150.12 (4°)

JOHN WHITAKER (fl. 1818)
The Seraph, a Collection of Sacred Music, Suitable to Public or Private Devotion, London, 1818
REFERENCE: Bentley 512
PROVENANCE: Gift of Charles Ryskamp
M2136/S43/1818

ROBERT JOHN THORNTON (1768–1837)
The Pastorals of Virgil, London, 1821
REFERENCE: Essick, *Commercial*, no. LIII
B1978.43.1720–1721

The Wood Engravings of William Blake for Thornton's Virgil 1821, London, 1977.
17 wood engravings reprinted from the original blocks
B1978.43.1586–1602

RELATED MATERIAL

WILLIAM BLAKE
A Descriptive Catalogue of Pictures, Poetical and Historical Inventions, Painted by William Blake in Water-Colours, Being the Ancient Method of Fresco Painting Restored, London, 1809
Letterpress
SPINE: 7½ in. (18.4 cm)
REFERENCE: Bentley J
PROVENANCE: Possibly one of four copies bought by Henry Crabb Robinson (1770–1850) from the artist on 23 April 1810 and given by Robinson to William Wordsworth (1770–1850); Bernard Buchanan MacGeorge (?1845–1924), by 1892 (Sotheby's, 1 July 1824, lot 124, bt. Dobell); (Maggs, 1924), from whom purchased by Willis Vickery (American Art Association–Anderson Galleries, 1 March 1933, lot 17, bt. Newton); Alfred Edward Newton (1864–1940) (Parke-Bernet, 17 April 1941, lot 149, bt. Gannon for Mrs. Paul Mellon).
B1978.43.1418

JOHN LINNELL (1792–1882) and his circle, after William Blake
Illustrations of the Book of Job (The New Zealand Set), after 1825
22 watercolors with pen and black ink, on 22 sheets
Various dimensions

REFERENCE: Butlin, pp. 409–410
PROVENANCE: Probably John Linnell (1792–1882); his pupil, Albin Martin (b. 1813); his daughters, Miss Fanny Martin and Mrs. E. J. Hickson (Sotheby's, 17–21 December 1928, lot 139, bt. Wells); Gabriel Wells (1862–1946); Philip Hofer (1898–1984), by 1933 to 1941, from whom purchased through (Thomas J. Gannon) by Paul Mellon, 1941.
B1992.8.7 (1–22)

Anonymous nineteenth century, after William Blake
Songs of Innocence and of Experience, c. 1808
54 watercolors with pen and brown ink, on 54 leaves (with a letter from Samuel Rogers)
SPINE: 8⅛ in. (20.6 cm); sheets: 7¾ × 5 in. (19.7 × 12.7 cm)
REFERENCE: Bentley, *Supplement,* Alpha, pp. 132–133
PROVENANCE: Possibly C. P. Burney; John Leigh Phillips (1761–1814); his son, John Phillips of Childwall; his daughter, Miss Caroline Phillips, by 1867; her nephew, Gilbert Phillips, to c. 1930; Anonymous (Christie's, 25 July 1958, bt. Stonehill for Paul Mellon).
B1992.8.14 (1–54)

JOHN FLAXMAN (1755–1826)
Portrait of William Blake, c. 1804
Graphite
8 × 8⅛ in. (20 × 20.5 cm)
REFERENCE: Keynes, *Portraiture,* p. 120, pl. 5
PROVENANCE: Ann Flaxman (née Denman, d. 1820), 1798; her husband, John Flaxman (1755–1826) (Christie's, 1 July 1828, lot 85, bt. Clarke for William Beckford); William Beckford (1760–1844); his daughter, Susan, Duchess of Hamilton; by descent to Sir Douglas Douglas-Hamilton (1903–1973), 14th Duke of Hamilton, from whom purchased by Paul Mellon, 1966.
B1992.8.11 (59)

GEORGE RICHMOND (1809–1896), after FREDERICK TATHAM (1805–1878)
William Blake in Youth and Old Age, c. 1830
Graphite with brush and brown ink
13½ × 10½ in. (34.3 × 26.7 cm)
REFERENCE: Keynes, *Portraiture,* p. 144, pl. 41
PROVENANCE: Probably Catherine Blake (1761–1831); Frederick Tatham (1805–1878), from c. 1831, and bound by him with *Jerusalem* (Copy E); George Blamire (?1788–1863) (Christie's, 6 November 1863, lot 213, bt. Daniels); William Fuller Maitland (1813–1876), to 1876; Anonymous (Christie's, 1 June 1887, lot 225, bt. Quaritch); (Bernard Quaritch) from whom purchased by Gen. Archibald Stirling of Keir, c. 1893; his son, Col. William Stirling, by whom sold through (Scribner's, 1952) to Paul Mellon.
B1992.8.1 (101)

GEORGE RICHMOND (1809–1896), after FREDERICK TATHAM (1805–1878)
Portrait of Catherine Blake, c. 1830
Graphite
13½ × 10½ in. (34.3 × 26.7 cm)
REFERENCE: Keynes, *Portraiture,* pp. 153–154, pl. viii
PROVENANCE: Frederick Tatham (1805–1878), from c. 1840, and bound by him with *Jerusalem* (Copy E); George Blamire (?1788–1863) (Christie's, 6 November 1863, lot 213, bt. Daniels); William Fuller Maitland (1813–1876), to 1876; Anonymous (Christie's, 1 June 1887, lot 225, bt. Quaritch); (Bernard Quaritch) from whom purchased by Gen. Archibald Stirling of Keir, c. 1893; his son, Col. William Stirling, by whom sold through (Scribner's, 1952) to Paul Mellon.
B1992.8.1 (102)

FREDERICK TATHAM (1805–1878)
Life of Blake, c. 1832
Manuscript
REFERENCE: Bentley, *Records,* 507–535
PROVENANCE: Frederick Tatham (1805–1878), from c. 1832, and bound by him with *Jerusalem* (Copy E); George Blamire (?1788–1863) (Christie's, 6 Novemeber 1863, lot 213, bt. Daniels); William Fuller Maitland (1813–1876), to 1876; Anonymous (Christie's, 1 June 1887, lot 225, bt. Quaritch); (Bernard Quaritch) from whom purchased by Gen. Archibald Stirling of Keir, c. 1893; his son, Col. William Stirling, by whom sold through (Scribner's, 1952) to Paul Mellon.
B1992.8.16

Anonymous nineteenth century (formerly attributed to William Blake)
God Creating the Universe, c. 1800
Pen and brown ink and graphite
9⁵⁄₁₆ × 13 in. (23.6 × 33.2 cm)
REFERENCE: Geoffrey Keynes, *Drawings of William Blake, 92 Pencil Studies* (New York, 1970), no. 6, repr.
PROVENANCE: Thomas E. Lowinsky; his son, Justin Lowinsky, from whom acquired by Paul Mellon, 1963.
B1977.14.6009

REFERENCES

Bentley
Bentley, G. E., Jr. *Blake Books*. Oxford, 1977.

Bentley, *Supplement*
Bentley, G. E., Jr. *Blake Books Supplement*. Oxford, 1995.

Bentley, *Records*
Bentley, G. E., Jr. *Blake Records*. Oxford, 1969.

Butlin
Butlin, Martin. *The Paintings and Drawings of William Blake*. 2 vols. New Haven and London, 1981.

Bindman
Bindman, David. *The Complete Graphic Works of William Blake*. London, 1978.

Easson and Essick
Easson, Roger R., and Robert N. Essick. *William Blake: Book Illustrator*. 2 vols. Normal, Ill., 1972–1979.

Essick, *Commercial*
Essick, Robert N. *William Blake's Commercial Book Illustrations: A Catalogue and Study of the Plates Engraved by Blake after Designs by Other Artists*. Oxford, 1991.

Essick, *Separate Plates*
Essick, Robert N. *The Separate Plates of William Blake: A Catalogue*. Princeton, 1983.

Keynes, *Portraiture*
Keynes, Geoffrey. *The Complete Portraiture of William and Catherine Blake*. London, 1977.

Keynes and Wolf
Keynes, Geoffrey, and Edwin Wolf 2nd. *William Blake's Illuminated Books: A Census*. New York, 1953.

SELECT BIBLIOGRAPHY

Bentley, G. E., Jr. *Blake Records Supplement*. Oxford, 1988.

Bindman, David. *Blake as Artist*. New York, 1977.

———. *William Blake: His Art and Times*. New Haven, 1982.

Bindman, David, ed. *Color Versions of William Blake's Book of Job Designs from the Circle of John Linnell*. London, 1987.

———. *Blake's Illuminated Books*. 6 vols. London: Tate Gallery and William Blake Trust, 1991–1995.

Damon, S. Foster. *A Blake Dictionary: The Ideas and Symbols of William Blake*. Providence, 1965.

Eaves, Morris. *William Blake's Theory of Art*. Princeton, 1982.

———. *The Counter-Arts Conspiracy: Art and Industry in the Age of Blake*. Ithaca, 1992.

Erdman, David. *The Illuminated Blake*. London, 1975.

———. *Blake: Prophet Against Empire*. Princeton, 1977.

Erdman, David, ed. *The Complete Poetry and Prose of William Blake*. Berkeley, 1983.

Essick, Robert N. *William Blake, Printmaker*. Princeton, 1980.

Essick, Robert N., and Morton D. Paley. *Robert Blair's* The Grave *Illustrated by William Blake*. London, 1982.

Essick, Robert N., and Donald Pearce, eds. *Blake in His Times*. Bloomington, 1978.

Frye, Northrop. *Fearful Symmetry: A Study of William Blake*. Princeton, 1947.

Gilchrist, Alexander. *Life of William Blake*. 2 vols. London, 1863.

Keynes, Geoffrey. *A Study of the Illuminated Books of William Blake, Poet, Printer, Prophet*. New York, 1964.

———. *William Blake's Water-Colour Designs for the Poems of Thomas Gray*. Paris, 1971.

———. *Blake: Complete Writings*. Oxford, 1979.

———. *The Letters of William Blake*. Oxford, 1980.

Lindberg, Bo. *William Blake's Illustrations to the Book of Job*. Abo, 1973.

Paley, Morton. *William Blake*. Oxford, 1978.

———. *The Continuing City: William Blake's Jerusalem*. Oxford, 1983.

Ryskamp, Charles. "Paul Mellon and William Blake." In *Essays in Honor of Paul Mellon, Collector and Benefactor*. Washington D.C., 1986.

Tayler, Irene. *Blake's Illustrations to the Poems of Gray*. Princeton, 1971.

Vaughan, Frank. *Again to the Life of Eternity, William Blake's Illustrations to the Poems of Thomas Gray*. Selinsgrove, 1996.

Viscomi, Joseph. *Blake and the Idea of the Book*. Princeton, 1992.